Spellbound

The Secret Grimoire
of Lucy Cavendish

ROCKPOOL

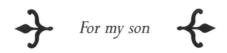

For my son

Lucy Cavendish is a true free spirit: a Witch and writer whose works are trusted and enjoyed around the world. An exciting voice in the field of inspiration, she is loved for her vision, compassion, wisdom and humour and has that rare ability to connect deeply with her readers.

Lucy's work is notable for its breadth and depth of knowledge on sacred rites and sites, magickal history, witchcraft, folklore, alternative spiritual practices and intuitive traditions. Her original creations have struck a chord with contemporary seekers who are ready to create lives of courage, spiritual adventure and magick.

Lucy's books and oracle decks are available in many languages, and she's a popular guest on television programs such as *Studio Ten*, *The Project* and *The Morning Show*. When she's not writing for or recording her popular podcast The Witchcast you'll find her drinking tea, surfing in the ocean or wandering deep within a faery forest.

You can discover more about Lucy by visiting her website, www.lucycavendish.com.au, or finding her on social media. You can also listen to The Witchcast, which is available wherever you get your podcasts.

A Rockpool book
PO Box 252
Summer Hill, NSW 2130
Australia

rockpoolpublishing.com
Follow us! f ⊙ rockpoolpublishing
Tag your images with #rockpoolpublishing

First published in 2013 as *Spellbound* under ISBN 9781925017151

This edition published in 2023 by Rockpool publishing
ISBN 9781925924534

A catalogue record for this book is available from the National Library of Australia

NATIONAL LIBRARY OF AUSTRALIA

Design by Sara Lindberg, Rockpool Publishing
Illustrations on p. 44 amd 52 by Kel Flowers

Printed and bound in China
10 9 8 7 6 5 4 3 2

Contents

INTRODUCTION

Ten years ago I was about to see this secret Grimoire of mine launched into the world. It was thrilling, and also a little nerve-racking and very exposing. There's a reason many Witches wait till they die before they share; perhaps it's because criticism can't touch them in quite the same way on the other side. However, I had really thought through that concept of waiting and I had a conviction that waiting and secrecy were not of great value compared with sharing and collaborating. I wanted to open the books to you all, for what the books had written within them had been of the greatest and most joyful help to me. And so I hope – so I trust – she has been to you.

And now here we are, within the gateway to a new world. What can continue to guide, heal and help us? What can help us imagine ourselves? What will empower us or reshape us? For me that has always been magick, put into personal practice and personal and collective service.

Spells and what they can do for us in terms of our personal growth, self-belief and, most importantly, our connection to the natural world are more needed than ever before. At their heart they only require our time and dedication. They are a way to generate, direct and sustain our personal energies to weave lives of beauty amid the challenges, to gather up the torn fragments of confidence and power and fortitude after loss and recreate the sacred heart of our own selves in new ways.

In the past 10 years we have grown as humans. We are becoming more open to a fluidity of form and gender, we are embracing differences that once were considered wrong and we are creating, imagining, working with technologies to attempt to give humans and all the life forms on this blue and green planet the greatest chance of moving into a future. Traditional religions, as with politics, seem more like archaic bureaucracies filled with hollow beliefs. The churches people once attended each Sunday are being converted into homes, and many people profess to believing in nature.

We are becoming Witches. Many crave more than ever the kiss of magick, the ecstasy of the full moon, the embrace of old trees and the wild sea salt spray of the ocean's waves of energy. We long for spirit but we no longer want, nor will we tolerate, a structured, distanced, wealthy religion that serves up more rules, more unbearable restrictions, more self-condemnation. It seems that we are finally done with such empty things.

That brings me to the magick, which belongs to no one and thus to all, the laws of which are those of the living and growing world and a force that makes sense of the splendid peculiarities of this life and its wondrous delights.

Reading back through *Spellbound* I realise that I, like you, have changed. My life has been transformed, sometimes willingly and sometimes with the pain of a difficult birth. Because of these changes I wondered if I would lack accord with what my younger self had written, but more often than not I found myself in agreement.

I am a believer in the need to shape and tend our consciousness. I believe that magick, through the working of trustworthy spellcraft, can be a conduit for that change and for that care of ourselves.

I believe – no, I utterly *know* that we crave the sacred, that we are thirsty for rites that satisfy a longing we see humans attempt to satiate with sex, the erotic, addictions to food, devices, people, avoidance, violence, shopping and money.

This Grimoire is a way to drink in, not *my* knowledge, but what is here, the ancient and the created, as sources and vessels for the energy you crave so deeply. This Grimoire offers ways to shape and reconstruct your life through the magickal dreaming of new possibilities, the eradication of the violent and harmful and the sustaining of a life of observance and a profound meaning that cannot be purchased. It can only be conjured.

Ten years ago this book came out, and it is a window into magicks that I trust to this day in this changed world. I have not changed the original text.

We are all changing and evolving, yet *Spellbound: The Secret Grimoire of Lucy Cavendish* will keep being completely there for you, for all the changing times, for all your changing needs, to support an ever-changing you.

Be most blessed and so much love to you,
Lucy Cavendish, 2023

Merry Meet

Dear Spellcaster

This book you hold is based on many musings, notes, spellworkings, craftings, castings, magickal notebooks, spell diaries, books of shadows and light – a collection of Witches' works that were once called a Grimoire. I have kept many of my workings very quiet, believing as I do in the adage – to know, to dare, to will, to keep silent.

But I feel now it is time to open those pages and invite you to explore the magick of my own secret Grimoire.

Although I know this book has its own powerful energy, it most truly comes to life once you begin to work with the magick inside. It's beautiful to read about magick – inspiring and delicious and uplifting. But taking the next step and doing it is when lives begin to change. I urge you with all of my heart not just to read, but to do – activate the transformative power of magick for yourself. Cast the spells. Cast and learn your craft. Watch your life become the magickal experience it was always meant to be.

You deserve it.

Blessings, love and magick to you,

Chapter 1

Welcome to the Craft of Spellcasting

✳ What is a Spell? ✳

There is an immense natural power in the Universe that you are a part of. You were born with this natural power. What our modern world has done is harness these natural powers in many ways — electricity, solar power, digital technology — but there is a deep, deep force that has not been harnessed, which cannot be controlled, that flows through all of us. Why don't you feel this force? Because most modern humans are completely disconnected from their own power. And the secrets to working with this power have almost been lost.

Spells are a way of reintroducing you to that natural power that flows through everything, including you. Crafting and casting spells will help reintroduce you to that power source, reconnect you, and that powerful connection with natural energy will help you create a meaningful, magickal life.

✳ What is Magick? ✳

Magick is the art and the craft and the philosophy of understanding nature's powers and then working with those powers to create the results you want and deserve in your life. That means bending and shaping natural forces. It does not mean trapping them, or distorting them, or exploiting them. Magick has many laws and many rules (see page 9 for more information), but the most important truth about magick is that you are a living example of magick. Yes, you! Without a whole series of natural amazing forces, right timing, fate, destiny and cosmic alignments, you would not exist. And there has never been anyone just like you. Not any time now or ever again; you're a natural miracle. You're magick.

✳ BENDING AND SHAPING ✳ YOUR ENERGY WISELY

These are laws and rules that apply to magick and spellcasting, but don't ever let the fact that there are rules and laws stop you from casting! People can be fearful of spellwork as they worry about a natural kind of punishment or that they are playing with an energy they cannot control. This notion comes from those age-old religions that tell you that fire and brimstone will rain down on you if you are not 'good', all backed up by the myths put out by so very many films and the media. You have this natural power within you, and it is your birthright to learn how to work with it.

✳ RULES AND LAWS OF MAGICK ✳ AND WITCHCRAFT

The Law of the Threefold Return

This law states that what you send out will return to you multiplied times three. This is called the law of the threefold return. Therefore, we do not cast with unhealthy energy because that is how you are going to feel: three times as much as the person or situation you're sending it to.

Be Balanced When You Cast

The most important energetic law when preparing to spellcast is to be clean and clear in your energy. No matter how angry or upset you are, you always need to be in a state of balance and calm when you cast. What this means is no drugs, alcohol or coffee before casting – you want your connection to be clean. If your energy is not clear your spell won't be either.

The Law of Harm None

Doctors have this oath, and as spellcrafting is a kind of healing, and definitely a working with natural energy to create change in accordance with the will, it is not surprising that as we know how to use these powers we make a promise that when we use them we will do no harm. What this law means is no casting to harm or hurt, no matter what. Before you cast, always say to yourself, 'Harm none.' There is a famous magickal saying: 'And it harm none, do what ye will.' Let that be your guide.

Cast for the Highest Good of All Concerned

These words are often woven into a spell in order to ask the Universe to help the casting be of the greatest possible good to all who are going to be affected by the spell.

Love is the Law

If we are not going to do any harm, and if we truly wish for the highest good of all concerned, that means love is the law. Love of life, of ourselves, of the planet, of the deities, of the sheer visceral thrill of being alive. So, where does this leave the infamous cursing and hexing? Many Witches do hex – it can be an effective way to stop something that is worth this risky magick. Hexing can work with 'inanimate' objects – hexing a disease is one practice some Witches feel very comfortable with. For the purpose of this Grimoire we will first work with ways to banish, block, protect and change energy – without hexing. You will learn of the many magickal practices that deactivate the impact of negative people and improve difficult situations. We do not have to suffer bullies, nasty people, toxic gossip campaigns and all the petty little evils that come into play throughout our lives. The practices within this Grimoire won't hurt the person. You'll be taught to deflect your attention away from the person and turn the magick so it affects behaviour – including your own, which will be making a significant energetic contribution to the situation. You'll learn some strong, fast-working psychic self-defence moves too. These are fun, empowering and, most importantly, effective.

The Law of Free Will

When we cast, we never cast to interfere with another person's free will. So, for example, we do not cast to persuade someone to do something against their will. This is magickal malpractice, and yet it is frequently sought after. Never cast without another person's consent. Do not cast to get people back together against the will of one of the people involved. Another ground rule is to never cast a spell or send energies to another person without their consent. Even if you mean well and are sending good energy or light, it is an invasion of a person's spiritual space. Obey this law, and you will cast safely and effectively for many years to come.

Like Attracts Like

What we think, we become. What we believe, we create. What we work with in our spells, we develop an affinity for and a relationship with. If we wish to work magick, we must work with tools and ingredients that are like those we wish to create or attract. This law has been renamed in recent years, and is often referred to as the law of attraction. We attract what we are. Our energy dictates our experience. This is not new. It is ancient, and it is powerful.

Never Cast for Negative Outcomes

If you begin casting for vengeful, malicious, petty and especially spiteful, egoistic reasons the impact is rarely pretty – for anyone. If you make this your practice you will take the brunt of the effect of the spell. Your energy will become drained and your faith in your magickal practice and in yourself will be severely shaken.

These laws can daunt potential spellcasters fearful of making a mistake, who worry they may inadvertently create mayhem. Gently place those fears and anxieties aside. Together we can travel right inside the magick of the Universe, and learn to understand natural energies so you have the best possible spellcasting experiences. But you need to make a promise to devote some time to work out why you want what you think you want. You need to understand the energy around you and how you can bend and shape it with wisdom. Spellcasting is not a matter of dipping in, casting a spell, life is perfect. It's more a matter of understanding the energy and tapping into its powerful force to help you create your own special magick. A big key to tapping into this energy is being open and learning to see your world differently. Magickally you will learn to open your heart and your eyes to the wider world.

Spells and Witchcraft

S *pells are generally associated with magick and witchcraft. Both of these terms can be a bit confusing, so here is an explanation that will help you understand the background of spells.*

Witchcraft is a misunderstood word. 'Witch' is a variant on another old Anglo-Saxon word, 'wicce', and has a couple of meanings: first, wicce means wise; second, it means to bend and to shape. If you put these meanings together — to bend and to shape with wisdom — what is it that is being bent and shaped with wisdom? The answer is raw, primal source energy. The Universe is full of this magickal, powerful material. It flows and gathers around us in cycles, with every season, moon phase, eclipse, solstice, equinox and solar year. Witchcraft asks you to shift your focus to this primal energy, understand you are a part of it, reconnect with the power inside you and outside of you and begin to work with it. And one of those ways of working with it is spellcasting — to bend and shape, wisely, to sculpt your reality.

Chapter 2

A Little History of Spells

Let's look back at the history of spells before we move forward with changing your life. Sounds a bit boring to some of you, right? You're probably itching to cast a love spell, get the after-school job you want or blitz your exams.

Let's do a little warm-up first. At the risk of sounding like an old-fashioned teacher, it is an important thing to understand the past if you are going to get into your own spellcasting. The past is really important – if we don't understand it this is the point where our present can go wrong and it inadvertently messes with the future.

Spells take place in every moment. Never forget your every thought and word work on the principles of magick. To get started, you need to start at the very beginning on the fundamentals of spellcasting. If you do this warm-up first you won't get hurt, strained or put off by the energy kickback you're going to experience a couple of times and will need to get used to. If you keep going, though, you'll notice you get stronger and more versatile – and your life will become more and more amazing.

Having some knowledge about the history of how spells and magick have developed is very important. Knowledge will empower you when you get hit with the questions you're going to get hit with. (Yes, you will.) You need to know the why of what you're doing and you need to be informed, so you can really back yourself if people think you're playing at Harry Potter or you just watched one too many episodes of Charmed. *Taking this spell and magick business seriously and becoming involved is part of a long, proud and very worthwhile tradition. This stuff works; it changes you, makes you courageous. You deserve to be a courageous and empowered person, but you need to achieve this responsibly!*

Spells and magick have been a part of everything on the planet since we humans came to life. Animals have their powers and their magicks – and we'll learn how to work with those later. You have to be patient!

When we look at indigenous cultures around the world (the people who stayed living close to the earth and the cycles of the planet) they all have spells. And spells are really just a way of praying or asking for something we want to happen. Most people in ancient times weren't so different from us, but they had more practical issues to care about. They needed rain to help crops grow, they needed the animals they hunted to be plentiful because they were hungry. They had spells for fertility, because having babies kept the tribe going and kept them strong to carry on their traditions. They prayed to overcome enemies who wanted their hunting lands or their pastoral fields – all really big concerns and very important.

There are spells and magickal workings to work when young men come of age – around puberty – so that they could pass the test and become men without being disruptive and hurtful to their tribal leaders and their people. Same with young women – puberty arrived, and a whole new level of teachings took place, rituals and spells so they could take their place with the mature women and know the ways of the land, how to birth a child, how to raise crops, herb lore and reading the stars. People close to the land learned the ways of the animals, the plants, the seasons and the cycles of nature.

Within these cultures and communities there were special people devoted to spells and magick and ritual and they were often called wizards or priestesses or shamans or medicine men or women. There were many special activities that took place around what we call the 'teenage years' to prepare young people for the life that lay ahead of them. The focus of all these spells and magick was the good of the tribe and the health of the individuals within this tribe. This magickal connection to life and earth and cycles began breaking down when the 'civilisation' of societies began to happen.

The Greeks and the Romans were experts at changing the way people lived, by making certain communities become 'civilised'. They built empires, they conquered lands and people, mainly because the people they vanquished had something they wanted or needed – slaves, minerals, gold, tin, jewels, farming land. It's not so strange; it's still going on right now. The point I want to make here is that these cultures usually imported their own view of the world, and thus their own version of spellwork and magick.

The focus moved from natural forces – the ways of the animals and the plants and the birds and the sky and the weather and the land – to the personification of these forces in the form of what we began to call Gods and Goddesses. Tribes worked with these divine forces but, instead of seeing them as entwined with nature, some of these cultures saw them as above nature – like the Greeks and the Romans did. Their Gods and Goddesses were so cosmic in their scope that they lived elsewhere, in heaven-like places called Olympus. And humans had to start really working with these Gods by making them offerings. (For more information on working these different deities, please see Chapter 8.)

Offerings and What They Mean

Offerings are really interesting. Offerings are also very important and they tie right back into spells. If you have an opportunity to visit Bath in England, the Roman Baths museum has a collection of syncretic spells, cursing tablets and prayers written on pieces of lead to the Goddess Sulis (the Goddess of the hot mineral waters that flow there to this day). They are more than 1500 years old and they are wonderful to read – people were casting spells back then, asking the Goddess for help with stolen goods, with love, with defending themselves against an enemy or to get better after a sickness.

In the 800s in England there were lots of what we can call syncretic spells – spells that combine influences and ask for help from Nordic Gods like Odin, Archangels like Michael and Elves as well as the spirit of the land.

A Spell to Connect With Your Magickal Bloodline

Someone, somewhere in your family, maybe even thousands of years ago, has worked as a spellcaster, magician or healer. And they, and possibly many others, have a lot of help to offer you. This spell can help you reconnect with your magickally supportive and caring forebears.

Of course, many of us have ancestors who have not been very nice. Be assured this spell is cast to draw to you the wisdom and knowledge of those who worked in balance. This spell can also be very helpful when we find our own family doesn't seem to have much to offer us in the way of magickal support. Here's how to awaken your own ancestral powers.

YOU'LL NEED:

A little piece of your hair
A small fireproof dish or bowl to place burning candles or matches
A red candle (for the bloodline of your ancestors)
A white candle (for the relatives and ancestry of your past lives)

WHAT TO DO:

✹ Cast your circle.

✹ Burn the little piece of your hair. The smoke going up from it means the ancestors will recognise you. Make sure you have a fireproof dish and water ready just in case of flames. Light the red candle and say:

I light a candle to my ancestors
Blood of my blood, bone of my bone
Keepers of the magick of the line.

❋ Blow out the red candle and place the red candle and
piece of hair into the flameproof dish or bowl.
❋ Light the white candle as you say:

I light a candle to my ancestors of my spirit
Ancestors of spirit, ancestors of blood
Those who cast. Crafted. Healed and chanted
I ask that you stand by me, and ensure that my every wish granted
Be for the highest good of my ancestors past and future
Let me learn your lessons within
Share with me your wisdom and your gifts
Let me dream dreams of magick, knowledge and power
Bring this to me, in every hour
I thank you all, future, present and past
For sharing with me your experience vast
Aid me now, and when I cast
Show me visions, to help me see
A future bright and purposeful for me.

❋ Blow out the white candle and place it in the dish.
❋ Visualise a line of ancestors travelling out beyond you, standing
behind you. There are so many, all shadowed. One will step forward,
and their features and their energy will become more apparent to
you. Ask them their name. Ask if they are your ancestral guide.
❋ Ask if they have good intentions. If the answers satisfy you, go on
and ask them a question.
❋ Thank them and close circle.

Chapter 3

Spellcrafting Cycles and Magickal Timing

✳ The Timing of Spellcrafting ✳ and Casting

The spells within this Grimoire work because they give you a proven set of steps to follow. These steps are a code, or password, that unlock a source of natural power and energy. Once you're connected you can direct that energy, which will be made even more potent if you channel it in the right way, at the right time. A great proportion of effective spellcrafting and casting is knowing when to cast for what it is you want to create in your life.

It's a little like being a great gardener – gardeners who are really talented and tuned in and knowledgeable do not try to grow jasmine in autumn or pumpkins in springtime. Spells work not because you're doing anything unnatural; they work because you're fertilising the possibilities the natural energy cycles are giving you. You're not going to try to work against nature – you're going to work WITH her, with her timing and cycles, and this is going to enhance the impact of your casting. Whenever you are preparing for your spellcasting, have a look at moon charts and write down in your Grimoire the time you have done your spells so you can see what times have worked and what times have not.

✳ Casting by the Moon ✳

Lunar phases have long been observed and held sacred. We have watched the tides ebb and flow, witnessed the response of the plants to the moonlight and noticed people's behaviour change at different phases of the lunar cycle.

When we craft and cast spells we nearly always do so at a time that is going to support the intentions and the purpose of the spell. There are important phases of each lunar cycle that we work with.

Dark Moon

This is the brief phase during which there is no visible moon in the night sky. The moon is always there, but at this phase she is not discernible to the human eye as she is turned away from the light of the sun. Dark moon is especially revered in many countries for cleansing rituals. The darkness brings up all that needs to be released, or ended, or completed before going into the next phase, that of beginnings and new growth.

CAST FOR: *spells involving going deep within, working with the aspects of yourself you wish to learn more about, banishing, clearing and deep, lasting protection. Understanding mysteries, connecting with deities who are considered dark – sometimes called the Dark Mother. This lunar phase gives us an opportunity to discover what has been hidden. A wonderful time to ask for secrets to be revealed, to wind up relationships and to release old and unwanted habits.*

New Moon

A new moon is when you can see that very fine silver crescent light up the night sky. The new moon is all about a building, a gathering of energy, and it is the time to start to sow the seeds of new projects, initiate ideas and relationships. It is the time to make a romantic advance, to initiate an exercise program. The energy at this time supports beginnings.

CAST FOR: *spells to begin a project, land a job, draw a new love, find a new home. Generally it is the right time to make any kind of change. It is gentle energy, so you must give any spell you work at new moon time to work before you see strong results.*

Waxing Moon

This is not a phase but a term used to describe the moon as she grows from dark to full – she waxes, grows bigger.

Waxing Quarter Moon

This is a phase when establishment, building and solidifying can take place. We can really begin to see results and observe growth by putting even more effort into our desires. At this stage, what we have cast for at the new moon will be growing, establishing itself and showing signs of manifesting.

CAST FOR: *building on the energy of new moon work or spells, reinvigorate current projects, for work, abundance, increase and commitment to relationships.*

Waxing Gibbous Moon

This is the time between the waxing first quarter and the full moon. There may be obvious, fast growth and more and more progress.

CAST FOR: *alliances, back-up, resources, storage, memory, provisions, expansion, evolution, progress, blossoming, extension.*

Full Moon

This is the time of the high tide of power. It is a time of fullness and intensity, when all that is being worked on, all that you are feeling and thinking and doing, will be amplified. It is very, very powerful. Some spiritual practitioners have suggested releasing at full moon. I strongly advise against this, as it is too volatile to release into. It is a time for fullness and, at such times, power can literally spill over.

CAST FOR: *increasing connection to lovers, gratitude, celebration, giving thanks, positive energy, divination, increase and amplification, generation of energy and absorbing energy, as this is extremely replenishing.*

Waning Gibbous Moon

Now, after the full moon, it is time to let go, to hold parties, to enjoy physical activity and dancing. It is the time between the full moon and the waning quarter moon. This is a time when rapid clearing and release can take place, with very obvious results.

CAST FOR: *reduction, diminishment, transformation, transmutation, dissolving negativity and difficult issues, release, clearing, cleansing, banishing.*

Waning Quarter Moon

This moon, like the first quarter moon, looks half full. It will again be useful for sending away, and it also is a kind of drawing out. So releasing negativity, losing weight and changing poor habits are favoured as energy is moving out – the tide is sucking out – so it is a purifying and releasing time.

CAST FOR: *clearly it is the time to send, to send away, release, detox and purge. It is the time to clean house, clean up our act energetically, to let go of bad habits.*

Waning Moon

This is a term used to describe the opposite phenomena – when the moon grows smaller – waning or diminishing in size from full through to dark again.

❋ SEASONAL TIMING ❋
Casting by the Wheel of the Year

Magick works with natural cycles of the earth and of the heavens. There are eight traditional festivals in modern magick. Four are associated with the changing of the seasons and four are connected to the Universe — two solstices, two equinoxes. Use these festivals as a guide to timing your spells. The Witches' Year is said to begin at Samhain, so this is where we will begin this guide to the Wheel of the Year.

Samhain (pronounced sow-en)
31 October–1 November in the northern hemisphere
30 April–1 May in the southern hemisphere

This is the Witches' magickal New Year. It is the time of the ancestors, when ghosts walk with us and when we acknowledge and remember those who have gone before us. It is a time of harvest and a time to light the darkness, and we begin to make preparations for the cold times coming. It has been adopted by popular culture and is known as Halloween, a variation of the old name All Hallows' Eve.

This is a strong time for candle magick, scrying, divination to forecast for the year ahead and connecting with ancestors. It is also a perfect time to practise your mediumship skills. If you wish to revisit the connection to ancestor spell (see page 18), this would be the perfect time.

CAST FOR: *finding a mentor, guide or benefactor as older, wiser energies can be trapped at Samhain.*

Winter Solstice – Yule
20–23 December in the northern hemisphere
20–23 June in the southern hemisphere

This is the longest night of the year – the time of the greatest darkness and of severe cold in many lands. The energy is slow, internalised and withdrawn. It is a time of incubation, hibernation and conserving energy. At the solstice, great celebrations were held through Northern Europe to call the sun back to life and warmth. Many ancient sacred sites were built to ritually honour and observe the solstices – and observation of the winter solstice, the time of rebirth after the death of the cold time, is considered by many to have been one of the primary purposes of Stonehenge. This is a time for candle magick, rebirthing, beginning the process of recovery after healing, divination for the future, gratitude and giving thanks.

CAST FOR: *if you are feeling lost, for you find your way through the darkness. Clearing of negativity and space clearing can also be worked with.*

Imbolc
1–2 February in the northern hemisphere
1–2 August in the southern hemisphere

This is a festival of growth, mothering, young life and nurturing the tender newness of the coming spring. Imbolc is an old Gaelic word that means 'ewe's milk', which relates to the birth of baby animals at this time. It is a fresh, invigorating and blessed festival. Because of the newness there is an innocence and a heightened sensitivity to the energy. It has a pure, sweet quality.

CAST FOR: *the future, new life, young ones, hopes, dreams, kindness and care, to be comforted, for mothers and parents, for teachers, counsellors and carers, change and education. To create optimism, self-love, tenderness and new romance.*

Spring Equinox – Ostara

20–23 March in the northern hemisphere
20–23 September in the southern hemisphere

This is a traditional northern hemisphere and Nordic celebration of fertility, abundance and new life. It is named for and devoted to the Goddess Ostara. It is linked to maturation, development, coming of age and initiation and is a joyful, hopeful time. As it is an equinox, the light and the dark are in perfect balance of equal duration, with the light growing stronger from the next day forth. So it is a celebration, too, of warmth. Many of its ancient traditions have been worked into Christianity's rites of Easter – a direct reference to Ostara's name. The eggs, the hare who brings them and the sweetness of chocolate and treats are all traditionally the gifts of this kind and lovely Nordic lunar Goddess.

CAST FOR: *emotional balance, anything at all to do with equality and fairness, sexuality, physical strength and fitness, health and well-being, justice, education, fair dealing, abundance, friendships, physical makeovers, beauty, gardening and attraction.*

Beltane

30 April–1 May in the northern hemisphere
31 October–1 November in the southern hemisphere

This is the highly sexual fertility festival of the Ancient Celts, a festival that means 'bright fire' that will relight the fire within you when you observe its magick. This is the traditional time for handfastings, or pagan weddings. It is a celebration of beauty, sensuality and desire. Beltane is a purifying festival. When, finally, the cold days had departed, animals could be moved into the higher paddocks to graze and spend time outdoors, bringing freedom and freshness. The fires that burned at this time lit up lovers meeting in the flower-filled fields. Today, as the world about you warms, you will feel inspired to dance, laugh and enjoy friendship and even fall in love.

CAST FOR: *attracting a love or lover who is committed and extremely attracted to you. To focus on your physicality, your health, your desirability and power. It is a time to dress up and play, rearrange your social life, make new friends and have flirtatious fun. It is a time of abundance, good fortune and prosperity. Spells cast to attract these will be highly favoured while Beltane's intoxicating energy holds sway.*

Summer Solstice – Litha

20–23 June in the northern hemisphere
20 23 December in the southern hemisphere

This is the festival of the faeries – Litha is intensely joyous, celebratory and full of light. It celebrates and marks the longest day of the year and it gives us all the opportunity to relax, bathe in the warmth, have plenty of time to ourselves and to spend with friends, play music, dance and be enchanted by the full flower of summer. It is a festival that encourages us to slow down and relax, sunbathe, stretch and give thanks for the simple joy of being alive under summer skies.

CAST FOR: *physical strength and health, creativity, inspiration and friendships. Parties thrown at this time are all magickal. Good fortune is more easily activated and vitality and play are also encouraged. You will have strong connections to plants, trees and crystals. You are more telepathic at Litha, more relaxed, like a blossom opening to the sun. Take good care of yourself as there can be a tendency to overdo celebrations.*

Lughnasad

1–2 August in the northern hemisphere
1–2 February in the southern hemisphere

As the dark lengthens it is time to harvest and give thanks to the Universe for what we have created – to be grateful. This is a time of balancing the efforts we have made with the enjoyment of what we have created – to celebrate the light that remains, to make the most of every moment before darkness falls. It is when Lugh, the Celtic God of Light, was honoured, and as he is also a God of many talents we attempt to do as much as we can at this busy time. We enjoy the bounty of our good fortune at this time, but put what we need away for the cold times are ahead. We also share, because when we have good fortune we must share it with others. We also resolve disputes at Lughnasad.

CAST FOR: *destiny, height of maturity and growth, peaks and pinnacles, luxury and comfort, cleansing and preparation, planning. It is a time to consider your future, plan and get organised, and to mend relationships or end them peacefully.*

Autumn Equinox – Mabon

20–23 September in the northern hemisphere
20–23 March in the southern hemisphere

This is the time of the descent into darkness, to strengthen ourselves: to make sure we are well physically and mentally and to ready ourselves for winter. As the dark grows and lengthens there will be changes, even separations. We are asked to be more responsible, serious, earnest and honest with ourselves. We must become leaders, to begin to think for ourselves and to rely on others. This is a time of complexity, as the days have this one last moment of balance before the dark consumes the light once again.

CAST FOR: *dedication, energy, independence, intelligence, practicality, study, qualifications, self-improvement, higher standards and making peace. It is a time for justice, to air grievances and to be sure we know where we stand with others before making commitments.*

GRIMOIRE EXERCISE

Beginning at the next dark moon, keep notes in your Grimoire for each of these moon phases and for these festivals of the Wheel of the Year. Make a note about how you feel, what the energy seems like and any impact it seems to be having on you. Spend some time outside, in moonlight, as much as possible. Try meditating with the moon and see what kind of information comes through to you. You may wish to invest in a crystal, such as moonstone or selenite, both of which contain and hold lunar energy, which you can direct in future spellwork. This is not an intellectual exercise; this is pure energy work. The more time you spend with the moon, the more connection you will feel to Luna's bright magick.

Chapter 4

Intent is Not Everything

Do you really need to actively create magick in your life? Why can't you just trust in the Universe and know all will be well?

Well, of course you can. But why not enter more fully into life?

There have been long and very philosophical discussions about spellwork, times when spellcasters gather to thrash out their thoughts around magick. The saying 'intent is everything' is something that comes up again and again in all those discussions.

Here is my take on this. Intent is vital, but it is not everything.

You see, some magickal workers feel very strongly that they need absolutely nothing to create a spell or to work and cast a spell or to bring something desired through into reality. Nothing except for their intention.

✷ THE MAGICK OF COMMITMENT ✷ AND ACTION

Without your commitment to gathering your ingredients, learning and studying and casting you only have the strong desire to do something. When your desire teams up with your commitment and your action, then you begin to create magick.

For example, if you have a powerful desire to get fit, strong and run faster, the sheer desire for that is not enough on its own. Nor is an entire gym full of equipment. None of that matters unless you translate that desire into its next stage – ACTION. And then, unless you follow through and recommit again and again, you will not see any significant changes take place. It is the same with magick in so many ways. You can buy all the supplies and have all the good intentions, but it is your actions that will create your results. You've got to really grow that strong, determined heart. That's when you'll see your life begin to change in so many ways that you'll be excited at your results and motivated enough to keep going.

So, the answer to the question I also get asked, which is 'Do I really need anything at all?', I think, yes, you do. You need to be grounded. You need to be dedicated. You need to action your intentions to create real magick.

A balance between going overboard with supplies, and overdoing the spellwork for say three weeks and then letting it go altogether, is the way to go. It doesn't really matter if you do one enormous spell that sets you in the right direction if you don't continue with the real point of all this, which is maintaining a healthy and strong connection to your centre and to your magickal nature. This is a path for life.

✳ THE MAGICK OF SILENCE ✳

What is the difference between wishing, spellcasting and creating? Well, making wishes can be very powerful, but they are very different to spellcasting and crafting.

If you yearn for something with all your heart and soul and follow through with action and commitment, this is the same as wishing, a close second to spellcasting. And remember that with any wishes you make (such as when you blow out your birthday candles), keep your wish to yourself, as talking about your wishes often fools you into thinking that you have already done the work. Your power diminishes.

To be kind of short and sweet about it, do NOT talk about your spellwork, except to maybe a couple of supportive friends or mentors. Trust me on this. Plenty of people will find your spellcrafting practice funny or silly or weird and you do not want to waste your precious and powerful and beautiful energy explaining yourself. It is counter-productive and it can sow doubt in your mind — and your mind is often where the magick begins. Don't pollute your thoughts with other people's doubts, opinions and judgements. Keep your own counsel and have faith.

To help you find the magick of silence, take a look at Chapter 9 on creating a sacred space for spellcasting.

Trustworthy
Magickal Partners

*K*nowing you can chat openly with a couple of people, trusted ones,
who are probably on the same or a similar path to yourself is
magickally helpful — and it can help you stay accountable. You can't
just say what you're going to do; often true friends will check in
with each other and compare notes on their results, giving advice to
each other about where they could have strengthened their results.
This doesn't happen easily or often, but when you encounter and
develop and nurture friendships like this it is worth treating them
well, and doing your best to maintain them. Friendships grow with
shared experiences and open-hearted generosity, listening and sharing.
They do not work well with power plays and boasting, so choose your
magickal friends carefully. The loneliness of doing this work can
sometimes drive us to attach closely to the first magickal people
we meet, but do be careful. It is worth taking your time
and developing true Witchy friendships that last.

❋ MANIFESTING: USING THE ❋
MAGICK OF YOUR MIND

*M*anifesting is another word that is used in a lot of magickal and spiritual
circles these days. In fact, it is used so often people hardly ever stop

to wonder what it means. 'Manifest' comes from the Latin noun *manifestare,* meaning an object, action or presence. To manifest is to clearly and unquestionably show, reveal, produce or display the existence of something.

Although the word began to be associated with spiritualism in the 1800s, when spirit beings and ectoplasm began to manifest during séances, the use of the word was made popular by Louise L. Hay in the 1980s. Hay was a renowned metaphysical teacher who believed she cured her cancer by finding the connection between the part of the body affected by the cancer and her mind. She decided to shift the way she thought, and in time her body grew stronger and healthier. She believed she had manifested cancer with her thoughts. She manifested health by changing her thoughts. She was a very wealthy lady with a huge publishing empire. What really counts in this example is that Witches and spellcasters have known for a very long time that the way in which you think, and what you think about, will have a direct impact on what you do and how you behave. This, in turn, will create your reality. What you think about, you create. There is an unbreakable connection.

So become aware of your thoughts. For the next seven days, make a note of the thoughts that take place and the clusters of thoughts you have. Write these thoughts down in your Grimoire so that you can track what you say to yourself or what you think. You will be able to see what are your most frequent thoughts. For example, one of my common thoughts that I am working on at present is 'I'd better . . .'

I also noticed when I first started with this exercise that when I did something I thought was 'wrong' I would call myself a name, like 'idiot'. I was also very, very sensitive to other people and their approval – for me, not fitting in was a big deal, and I was always searching for ways to find a safe place for myself in groups. I had really good friends but I did not seem to have a lot of confidence in other people and their friendship, so I needed to change how I thought and behaved.

Have a look at chapters 6 and 7 to find out about working alone and with patience and trust to help give you confidence when spellcasting.

GRIMOIRE EXERCISE

❋ *Becoming Aware of Your Thoughts* ❋

Here is your exercise for this chapter. It's about understanding your self-talk and where it comes from. Keep notes of how you speak to yourself over seven days. Whenever a really powerful thought comes up – whether you say it out loud or just to yourself – make a note. Don't go crazy with this; you just need to catch those really strong thoughts. If they're strong enough for you to notice them it's likely you're saying them at a subconscious level a lot, and that ultimately programs you to think a certain way, which becomes a pattern. This changes your energy and it begins to come true because you've made it your reality.

Once you've got those predominant thoughts written down, give yourself some space to think this over by asking yourself the following questions:

* ❀ Do any of the phrases I'm using sound kind of familiar?
* ❀ Did anyone else in my family ever say this to me?
* ❀ Am I clear on the fact that saying this is like programming myself to produce exactly that outcome?
* ❀ Is this what I want to create?

I had a lot of issues with the big, positive affirmations used by the New Age community. I could not shift my thinking so radically – for example, I could not confirm confidently 'I am wealthy' when in truth I was struggling financially. For me, it felt untrue. I wanted to change my thoughts and be truthful in order to do better and build my strengths, rather than ignore my weaknesses and avoid hard truths. I wanted, simply, to find more productive and encouraging and constructive ways to talk to myself so I would be confident enough to effectively change my life.

You may discover a lot about yourself when you do this exercise. You'll also start to change when you apply the change in the thought. Even if it feels weird or egotistical at first, keep it going. After one moon cycle a really good portion of that new thought – or alternative thought – is going to embed itself in your mind, your physicality and your energy field. Being aware of your thoughts is essential for your spellwork as it will raise the quality of your energy. It can also change your life.

☀ RAISE THE QUALITY ☀ OF YOUR ENERGY

Raising the quality of your energy will improve the quality of your reality. Your energy and its characteristics are going to influence, almost dictate, the quality of your experience. Now, if you are wanting to craft and cast a spell to attract and draw a relationship, for example, but you are holding on to some very powerful thoughts that negate that desire, you're going to stall and your spell is going to falter. It's never going to gain traction and it's going to take a few goes to really make any headway. Then when you get into the relationship your thoughts are going to sabotage it. Clean your kitchen – your mind – then cook – spellcast. It will create much better results and any efforts made will really take hold and move forward.

While completing this chapter I found scrawled in one of my old Grimoires from more than 20 years ago this saying attributed to Buddha: 'All that we are is the result of what we have thought. The mind is everything. What we think, we become.' And one more from the sixth-century Hindu prince who founded this philosophy that has influenced so many magickal practitioners: 'An idea that is developed and put into action is more important than an idea that exists only as an idea.' And that, I believe, is the difference. Thought is magickal. Intent is vital. But action empowers. Your most inspired intent needs to spring to life through action, and so it is with magick.

CHAPTER 5

The Elements of Spellcasting

✳ Building a Magickal Altar ✳

Magick brings us closer to the pure beating heart of your world, our world, the whole world. The closer you are to feeling that primal heartbeat the juicier, the keener, the tastier life gets. Spellwork creates a connection to the planet that makes you realise you belong. You feel safe, at home and protected. You will worry less about what others think and feel about you – you won't lose empathy and you won't stop caring, but you will stop worrying over issues that truly are a major drain on your life force. And that means you can achieve great things in your life.

It is a powerful magickal exercise to build an altar using objects that you find or collect. Be intuitive about this process. While it's great to collect a symbol for each element – earth, air, fire, water, spirit – it's more important that everything says something about the true you. So, perhaps beautiful flowers, herbs, some clear fresh water in a pretty cup, salt, symbols, candles and images that evoke a feeling of the sacred and a true sense of who you are becoming. Remember, being a spellcaster spiritually means connecting to the source. Your altar can reflect that.

For an altar, you simply need a space – it can be as large or as small as you wish. It's a beautiful place to keep oils and crystals, too. Images of inspirational people, mythological archetypes, Gods and Goddesses, you could include artists, poets, athletes, philosophers. What is important is that your altar and everything on it speaks to you about you and who you wish to become. Rework your altar whenever you feel you have changed.

Magickal Tools

*Y*ou may wish to keep your magickal tools on the altar. Take
your time collecting them. Here are some suggestions of tools
you can place on your altar:

❃ Cauldron: *this is associated with all elements as it can
hold all elements. It can be used for burning, for brewing potions
or for holding salt and earth. They have three legs and each leg
represents an aspect of the triple Goddess: Maiden, Mother and Crone.*

❃ Wand: *you can make your own wand simply by collecting fallen
wood from a tree you have a connection to. You can work with your
wand to direct energy and to cast circle.*

❃ Chalice: *can be used to hold sacred or blessed waters.*

❃ Candleholder: *safe and beautiful, they are a wonderful Witches' tool.*

❃ Candlesnuffer: *some spellcasters prefer to staunch or snuff the
candle either between their fingertips or with a snuffer. This is
believed to keep the energy with the spell rather than blowing it away.
I blow or snuff according to how the energy feels. I blow the candle
out when I feel the energy needs to be sent out into the world.*

❃ Athame: *the double-bladed Witches' knife is an important tool
for working with energy. It can also be used to cast circle. Some
spellcasters work with a sword, which is a stronger, more powerful
delineator of where energy begins and ends. It is often used in
energy surgery.*

✸ Casting a Magick Circle ✸

The casting of a protective circle is an important part of spellcrafting and magickal work. When we work magick we enter into a slightly altered state of consciousness. It is very subtle for some, while for others it can be almost a full trance. When in this altered state we require protection from unwanted and sometimes unhealthy energies that can be attracted to our energy, from which these energies can feed. The casting of a circle delineates a world between the worlds within which you can safely cast, craft, meditate and do your magickal work. This protective boundary, through which no harm can enter and manifest, is your sanctuary and your safeguard.

The circle is cast in the direction called deosil. This means sunwise – and sunwise is in fact different in the northern hemisphere and the southern hemisphere. While the sun rises in the east in both hemispheres and likewise sets in the west, the direction it appears to travel in is different. In the northern hemisphere the sun rises in the east then moves to the south (which is why the further south you go in the northern hemisphere the warmer you get). In the southern hemisphere the opposite applies – the sun rises in the east, then moves to the north.

This means that the deosil direction in the northern hemisphere is clockwise and in the southern it is anti-clockwise. We cast, or open a circle, in the deosil direction so it flows with the natural energy of the planet.

As an interesting aside, it also means that if clocks had been developed in the southern hemisphere they would have run in a different direction!

❉ Casting the Circle ❉

There are many ways to cast a circle, from the very simple to the very complex. Some spellcasters ensure they completely clear and bless the area in which they will work their spell before casting. Others simply begin after finding a place where there is good energy. Most often we will be doing this at home, so we need to be prepared to work with the space we have.

The wonderful thing about circle casting is that it can be done almost anywhere. The energy and magick travels within you and you carry this ability to create a safe, powerful and magickal space wherever you go.

* ❉ Stand facing the east. Raise your dominant or sending hand (the one you use to write or catch with) and extend it. (You may wish to use an athame or a wand or even a sword. I suggest beginning with your hand.) See either in your mind's eye or with your imagination a surge of energy extending in a line from your hand or your pointer finger. Now, you can choose the type of energy you are creating here, or as an exercise you can see the quality of energy that naturally comes from you. Notice the colour your energy has. Your personal energy will have its own quality, and everyone's energy, and thus everyone's circle, is slightly different.
* ❉ Remember to cast in the deosil direction. Standing on the spot, see this line of energy flow in a circle about you. Turn so that it completely surrounds you, flowing out of you. Ensure the circle is joined.

* When your circle joins up, it is cast. You may wish to widen your circle so it extends above you, below you and completely encloses you, becoming more of a sphere. Finally, your circle joins up.

✳ CALLING THE DIRECTIONS ✳
AND ELEMENTS

Traditionally spellcrafters often call in the directions and elements to join them in their magickal circle. It is a way of establishing where you are in the world and acknowledging the natural forces around you.

We also believe that there are guardians who care for each direction, looking after that part of the world and caring for the elements, creatures, energies and people that reside in that direction.

There are traditional directions where elements reside, and you can call them in from those or you can call them in geocentrically. Geocentric just means according to the land where you are.

So, here are the traditional northern hemisphere directions and the elements associated with them. These are often referred to as correspondents. Types of animals, types of tools and certain elements and energies are often considered to belong to each element.

Let's keep it simple to begin with and start with the elements.

* EAST — air
* SOUTH — fire
* WEST — water
* NORTH — earth

However, if you live on the east coast of Australia you may want to acknowledge the element that is actually most powerful according to that direction. So your elements and directions may look more like:

- EAST – water (for the ocean)
- NORTH – fire (as this is where it is warmest)
- WEST – earth (for the vast mountains and deserts that stretch to the west)
- SOUTH – air (for the great storms, the southerly busters that blow up the coast)

Whichever way you decide to cast, wherever you choose to acknowledge the elements and however you acknowledge the guardians of the directions, it is best to keep it simple at first. Over time, it can become richer, more personal, growing deeper. Initially, you can simply turn to face the direction and say:

Hail and welcome, guardians of the east. I call upon the element of water to join me in this circle now.

In time, you may want to add a few words about what water means to you, its cleansing abilities, and acknowledge any animals and deities associated with water that you would like to work with.

Try to align who and what you call in with the purpose and intent of your spells.

Remember to call to each direction and its element in turn, moving in a deosil direction to open. Circle casting nearly always begins in the east.

Following these simple steps can anchor and help you as you learn this art. The main point to remember and draw strength from is that you are first creating a protective boundary, then you are empowering it with magick by calling in the elements and directions, then you go about your work safely and supported.

✳ Closing the Circle ✳

Y ou will often see or hear closing the circle referred to as 'opening' the circle. In any case, when you have completed your work you bring your circle down. If you don't, your spell can remain in place, unresolved, and the magick will not be fully sent out into the world. You can also drag some of the energy around with you throughout the day or night, and magick is best begun and completed, so there is a clarity about it. We always must end, or close, as we began – strongly.

To close your circle, you turn to face the direction and element you last called. You're going to do exactly the same thing as you did when you cast your circle, only in reverse. So first you thank the last direction you called, thanking the guardians of that direction, thanking the element and saying 'Hail and farewell' (see the wording on page 47). Turn to the next direction, then the next, until you are at the east finally, and thank the guardians of the east and the element that resides there. Then standing, see the energy all about and around begin to shimmer and fade in the reverse direction to which it was cast. This closing direction is known as widdershins. Some spellcasters extend their hand (or athame or wand) and draw the energy back into them. I am far more inclined to let it transmute and be closed so that the energy can be absorbed into the world rather than reabsorbed into me!

✳ The Art of Magickal Dressing ✳

When we work spellcraft it can help to look the part. Although it does not matter in some ways, in others wearing certain clothes for certain practices can have a very real energetic impact.

There is the concept of robes. Now, you can be literal about this if you wish or you can think of the modern-day version I often see – the hoodie. If only hip-hop artists and UFC fighters realised how much they looked like druids in their snug work-out hoodies! The point is that a strong cape with a hood is very handy for several reasons. It is weather protective, so if you are working outside it will have an impact in that you won't get wet or freeze while casting your spell. Robes also provide a degree of anonymity – it's much harder to know who is outside at night working some magick when people cannot see you, your clothing or even your size or body shape or hair colour!

Robes cover you, shelter you and will help you feel very protected and strong. Also, if you choose to work with elements such as water, fire and air, obviously robes are going to help protect you.

A Link to a Magickal Past

Robes link you right back to longstanding magickal traditions. Whenever we see Witches or druids portrayed, they are often wearing robes. Somewhere along the line robes became more the domain of priests and monks, but the same principles apply. When we are doing certain sacred workings we wear certain clothing (and sometimes no clothing at all – your choice). Everything plays a part in the power it will give you and the energy it will promote or the energy it will suffocate. Some people just have one magickal outfit they wear for special times when they want everything to be lined up perfectly for their spellcasting. For others it becomes a matter of nearly everything being magickal to wear after a while. I'm kind of in that position myself now. It's harder for me to find clothing that doesn't have some kind of magickal memory attached to it. Because of how I live now nearly everything feels right to wear.

However, I do have some clothing that I wear often for ritual work or spellcrafting alone, and it does have a certain energy to it and has held on to the magick. I can feel this energy every time I put that particular garment on. It adds a little extra energy to the whole ceremony and helps me make the mental shift from this world to the next.

The Magick of the Crown Covering

When we work magickally, it can be considered to be good protocol to have the head covered – or to reveal the head at the right time. This really is not about drama or attempting to be theatrical, although having that cape or hooded robe really does put you in another frame of mind. Over time, as you do your magickal work your robes will take on the energy of the working you've been doing. The more positive and successful your magick, the more of this energy your clothing will store. For some people this becomes more and more important over time.

The Magick of Personal Meaning

It's probably best you choose something that really has meaning for you to create your own magickal clothing. For example, magick practitioners will sometimes stitch symbols into their robes or a number of knots or stitches that have important personal symbolism to them.

Sometimes magickal people inscribe their magick onto their body in the form of magickal tattoos. The history of tattoos is that they were most often marks of ancestry or protection, and this always had magickal significance. However, it is not always necessary to mark the body permanently, unless that is something you have thought about and made a very serious and responsible decision about.

You can inscribe a symbol for the purpose and duration of a spell on your skin in a subtle place on your body, while you are undergoing the working and changing the energy into your life.

You can use body paint, or make your own out of clay or henna to create the magickal results you wish to manifest into your life. The materials you use will have an impact on the spell you are creating. If you are wanting a strong impact I would be inclined to really ground the energy with the earth from where you live, which will also hold your energy.

Runic Symbols

Runes are and will be used in our magick. They are a form of written language developed by the people of the Norselands over 2000 years ago. They are symbolic and each rune holds within it many concepts and a great deal of energy. When you draw the rune on your skin or carve it into a candle you are really calling upon the energy held in the symbol to come to you to be of aid during your working. I do not feel you need to study the runes for years before you use them. However, working with respect and integrity — and also with humility — is important. Symbols take time to learn, and one of the best ways to learn is to begin, have patience and develop your knowledge slowly and practically.

Amulets and Symbols

Magickal amulets and symbols were widely used in ancient cultures, such as in Egypt and Mesopotamia. And you are not just tapping into the natural power: you're also having your spell fuelled by thousands of years' worth of belief in them. Belief creates energy. We have never really stopped using spells and magick. We just kind of pretend we don't believe.

But watch people! Will they walk under a ladder? Will they step on a crack in the pavement? Humans are believers, and what we believe in has power. We've believed in spells for a long long time, so when you cast and craft a spell you are tapping into an historic source of occult power.

The Eye of Horus

One symbol you can begin to use right away is the Eye of Horus. This has been used for thousands of years as a symbol of protection, wholeness and health. It is wonderful to use if you are feeling run down, hurt (emotionally and physically) or if you've been sick. If you have vague feelings of things being not quite right the Eye of Horus, or wedjat, can look out for you.

So, what is the Eye of Horus? In Egyptian cosmology (the way they believed the world and the planets and the whole natural thing hold together) Thoth healed the God Horus, restoring his missing eye, giving him back his external and internal sight and the gift of being able to look out for danger and opportunities. (These things are not as different from each other as you would think.)

Eye of Horus Protective Talisman

This is a very ancient and effective spell for protection, a variation on an Egyptian spell that we know an Egyptian woman named Helena cast around about 250 CE. This is a slightly more modern take, but the essence and power remain the same.

YOU'LL NEED:
Parchment (a teeny-tiny piece)
A pen with deep blue ink
A little bottle or a tiny glass tube
Some string or pretty velvet thread

WHAT TO DO:
❀ Write on the piece of parchment or thick paper, with deep blue ink write, small as can be:

Heal me
Look out for me
Warn me
Encourage me
Inspire me
Let all I see be clear
Give me no need to fear
Keep me safe from all harm
With this, my wedjat talisman charm
Bless me and protect me, Horus.

❋　Hold the bottle in your hands for a moment and really feel the protective love and energy of the Eye of Horus and say the words you have written down out loud three times with strength and conviction. Really give it some energy and intensity, so the energy and certainty you bring to your spell is infused into the parchment and the words go out into the Universe and Horus can hear you!

❋　Draw the Eye of Horus on the other side of the small piece of parchment.

❋　Roll this parchment up and pop it in the little bottle, tie the velvet ribbon or thread about the neck of the bottle and wear it about your neck or wrist for nine days.

❋　When you have done this, you may hang it on the door of your room, within your locker or off your bed – wherever you feel you most need protection and the magickal eye looking out for you.

❋　If you feel very seriously that you have suffered too much bad luck or that you are fragile, consider drawing the Eye of Horus on your body. The best place for this is on your back or between your shoulder blades, so literally Horus will 'have your back'. Ask a friend to help you.

❋　It is wise to say 'Thank you' to Horus often. Simply say, 'Thank you, Horus, for your watchful eye of protection. I will reinforce the spell and re-energise it, boosting its power and increasing your own belief and conviction in your safety.' That way, of course, your energy keeps on shifting and getting clearer, sounder, healthier and stronger, thus the safer and more protected you will be.

CHAPTER 6

Working
Magick Alone

M agick is not in any way supernatural, except in that you are developing something natural to a level that some see as extraordinary. It's not really. Put simply, it's about taking all that potential you have and developing it. This is as much a craft as it is an art, and it adds much beauty to the world.

It helps, always, when learning this craft to know who you are, to know what you are and to know why you arc. And in the end it will be up to you to find your own way into the Craft of the Wise, to make it your path, to work your magick. And many of you will be doing this alone.

Spellcasters who work alone are most often called 'solitaries'. They can move in and out of magickal groups, sometimes called covens or circles, but they tend to do their work on their own. If this is you, it is especially important for you to understand that you will need to be very dedicated.

Witchcraft and magick require practice and time. The living of it will be what gives your path, your spells, your rituals their power, energy and integrity. Small acts of magick each day over time will shift and change your energy, will give you a strength from deep within. It is not enough to dress up as a Witch, although clothing can hold and store energy (see Chapter 5). It is not enough to cast one spell. To be a spellcaster you must put your own self and soul into your magick, because being a spellcaster means being your own self. Spellcasters usually feel a connection with their planet and all beings on it. They also live from their wisdom, and they not only *believe* in magic, they create magick. A spellcaster can be anyone who follows this commitment. Everyone, in some way, has a little magick inside them, for all of us deep down have wondered if we can change things by willing them.

My practice is based on the idea this work is good for us, good for the soul, that it helps us connect deeply with the earth and the waters and the breath and the air and the fires. It means I must take responsibility and cease to fool myself about whether others are to blame. It requires even more responsibility when it come to casting because I acknowledge that what I do has an impact on myself and on the planet.

A Dedication Spell

This is a pledge you can make to yourself to help you stay on the right path.
It focuses your dedication to spellcrafting, casting and the working of magick.
If you are ready for this, you are ready to make a promise to yourself.

*I [your name here] learn of magick and spellcrafting and casting of my own free will, for
the good of my own self and for the highest good of all. I will observe the law. Do as you
will, but harm none. I will be free, and my intent will be pure.*
*I seek no power over another, only to work with the natural cycles and energies of the planet
in ways that create a beautiful life.*
*I promise to do no magickal work without consent unless there are extreme and extenuating
circumstances. Nor do I read people, or offer my observations without invitation or guidance.*
I understand the law of the threefold return — what I create resonates threefold.
*I understand that what is created in love, respect and power creates a vibrational field of
love, respect and power. I understand that the opposite is also true.*
I respect all life as sacred, and know that this earth and her inhabitants are sacred, too.
*I will honour the natural laws of creation, attraction and peace. I am now in the service of
magick for the highest good for all.*
I respect and allow differences. I will not judge, but I will discern.
*I thank the Universe, the God and the Goddess and myself for opening to me the
wonders of magick.*

❊ Find a place where you can be alone for about 20 minutes at least. Whether it is inside or outside or beautiful or everyday does not matter. What is of importance is that you have the space and privacy you require.

❊ Take your salt, incense or smudge stick, candle and some water you've blessed and consecrated.

❊ When you are calm, grounded and feeling like it is time, light your incense or smudge stick. Say:

As I do this I ask for the blessings of the air.

❊ Walk in a circle in the direction best for your hemisphere. For the northern hemisphere, walk clockwise. For the southern hemisphere, walk counter-clockwise. Let the incense or smoke from the smudge stick form a protective, enchanted circle around you.

❊ Ask for the blessings of the fire.

❊ Light your candle and walk in the same direction, creating in your mind's eye a wall of flame through which nothing that would do you harm can pass.

❊ Take up the water and walk in the circle, sprinkling it. Say:

I ask for the blessings of the water on this magick
I work this day.

*   Stand in the centre of this circle and read out the
words written on your parchment or paper.
*   Take a little time in the circle you have cast to think over these promises.
You may wish to spend some time simply communing with your own
Higher Self, which can often be activated during rites such as these.
Over time, if you begin to work with others you can adapt this simple
dedication ceremony so that you begin to connect your energy. Energy
raised with like-minded individuals in healthy rites can produce a great
deal of power and be very effective for healings and other spellworkings.

✳ CRAFTING AND CASTING SPELLS ✳ FOR OTHERS

I can guarantee this: if you are involved with magickal work, someone, at some stage, will come to you and ask for help. This is one of the great gifts of magickal work — you can help people. But this is also one of the downfalls of this work. You must learn to work within guidelines that ensure your magickal practice has integrity.

Spellworking for others is one of the most tricky and precarious areas of magick. I am so often asked if I can cast for another and get a particular result. I will only ever do this if the person themself asks directly for help and if it feels right. I am very cautious regarding casting for others. I have crafted spells for friends, but rarely have I cast for them. Casting for a friend might lead to them handing over their personal power, which will possibly jeopardise the friendship and their own destiny. If you do decide to cast for close friends always stick to the following magickal rules.

✻ *They must directly ask for you to cast or craft for them*

I tend not to offer people readings or insights or spellwork unless someone comes to me and asks. Why? Well, if you are pretty intuitive and you tend to see and feel and hear a great deal, you are going to receive messages and information and vibes from other people a lot of the time. If you spend most of your time relaying these messages to people, several things are going to happen. They're going to try to stay away from you. No one likes people constantly advising them. I had one friend who, when she was training to be a psychotherapist, managed to make every get-together a psychotherapy session. Now, it was kind of great — there I was, getting free counselling, but of course it was changing the dynamic of our friendship, putting her in the role of the professional and me in the role of someone who needed her help. I didn't ask for that help; psychotherapy had just become so fascinating and so amazing to her that all our conversations took that turn. And that injured our bond. It can also mean an imbalance can occur in the friendship.

❈   *Encourage others to help themselves*

If you start working spells and you have positive results and a friend comes to you for help, of course you should help them. But there is a real danger that a friend will give up all their power and hand it over to you and to the spell to fix them and their situation. Sometimes people put all their trust in you and do nothing to change their energy or take any action. They get a little result for a moment and then things go back to how they were, and then they claim your spell didn't work. And let's not even go into people who self-sabotage. This is why doing the work we spoke about way back in those early chapters is so important. If you cast for a person who has a mindset that is strictly 'nothing good ever happens to me', guess what? It becomes a self-fulfilling prophecy!

GRIMOIRE EXERCISE

✳ *Circle of Time* ✳

Think of time as a circle. The wheel of time is always turning, always returning to the same place. Think about the seasons, the moon cycles and the tides. There is an order and a rhythm to the Universe that cannot be understood or connected with if we think of time as a straight line, ever moving forward. Likewise, if we rush through most of our lives we miss some of the most beautiful gifts existence has to offer us. Good things take time. Magick works at that wise, cyclic and very natural pace. Patience, trust and timing will help your spells work.

Be aware of time and how you work with it. A thoughtful relationship to time is going to help you stay centred, connected and grounded when casting your spells, and as a result your spells will be effective.

CHAPTER 7

Patience and Trust are Magickal

Many people ask me, 'How long does it take for a spell to work?' This is a tricky question but it's also a very valid one. The length of time is going to vary from person to person and will depend on how you cast the spell, the clarity of your energy, your intent and the amount of follow-through work you do. The more patient you are and the more trust you pour into your energy around the spell, the more magickal your spell will be. Even though timing varies from spell to spell, for many spellcasters the impact is immediate and begins the moment the decision to cast, and to cast well, is made. With every action – from gathering water to lighting a candle – the magickal energy of your spell grows and gathers, ready to be directed towards your purpose. All this energy is generated before you have even cast your magickal circle. And when you go on to cast, then back up your spell with the energy of trust and patience, powerful results soon manifest.

It's easy enough to know whether a spell has worked. You may feel different immediately after casting your spell. That's because you have changed your energy. The results continue to build when you consistently align yourself to that changed energy. So, in a spellcasting like that, where the results are felt and your world changes, you could say that the spell worked right away. Now, the impact of other spells may begin to manifest very slowly, very subtly. If a spell's results are consistent over time or over several moon cycles and real clear change has been created it can definitely be said to have worked, but most spells with an outcome kind of purpose – for example, a spell to create a new job, a spell to become more abundant, a spell to attract new friendships – can take up to three moon cycles to work and their effectiveness will require persistent energy.

The working of magick and the casting of spells requires patience and trust, and the amount of time it may take for you to see results is also directly tied in to how you deal with this question of 'how long'. Some people cast beautifully and magick flows, but their doubts harm the spell. When they doubt they start to pick at the spell, worry at the magick. I feel it is best not to poke at the spell while it is tender and vulnerable. Imagine you've planted a seed. You've done all the work you need to — you've made the ground clear and rich and free of rocks and weeds. You've chosen your seed wisely, knowing why you want an apple tree or basil or to grow a tomato! You have chosen the right time to plant it, and so you did with lots of love and energy and good thoughts. But if you return to the tenderly planted seed and dig it up every few hours to see if it is sprouting, you will kill its growth with the glare of the light. So too is our doubt death to our magick.

✳ BELIEF IS AN ENERGY ✳

What every spell requires for clear, strong results is the quiet, strong, firm, even unshakeable belief that it is working. Tell yourself your spell is working. Do not allow doubt to enter your mind. That weed known as doubt can take root in the most unlikely places, so when it comes in clear it out right away.

It's held true in my life, and in the lives of many other people, that it takes one lunar cycle for anything to really change, to give change time to take root and to send its shoots up. Changing habits, changing lives takes time and persistence, retraining of your mind and consistent vigilance over your energy. Spells require the same kind of patience and dedication.

My rule of thumb with spells is when you are casting for big changes such as new jobs, homes and loves, give the spell time to work. Be really truthful about what you want and when you want it by because the Universe responds very well to being given clear energy and direction. Be very focused on what it is that you want and then leave it be, but feed the spell with your belief and with your follow-through actions. If you are looking for an after-school job then polish up a resume full of quiet confidence and really know what you have to offer. Walk in to any interview with strength and power, but with respect too. Your energy will attract what you have aligned yourself with. See yourself working in a job that pays you fairly and gives you the independence you're seeking.

When you affirm your spell is working, always do so in a positive way. For example, don't ever say 'I do not want a boss like that' or 'I hope I never have to go without again,' because your subconscious is really straightforward and it tends to hear everything as a 'Yes' statement. If you are asking to not get something, it won't really hear that. It's a bit like telling your dog you're not taking it for a walk. Your dog is only going to hear the crucial word 'walk' and respond to that! So you reframe those statements as 'I want a job with a boss who is flexible, understanding and who I can respect.' This will create better results than 'I do not want a horrible boss.' Frame it positively and strongly so your subconscious and the Universe are clear on what you want.

If you have patience and trust and if you frame your own thoughts so they support your spell, you will create magick that manifests at just the right time. Include the timing within the spell and be really determined to be on your own side and on the side of your spell. If you really feel something is off or that you've made a mistake you can go back to the beginning with your spellcasting easily enough. However, I would recommend that you think carefully before discounting any spell you have cast.

I have found that the more I work on clearing my own energy, through forgiveness work such as clearing any resentment, grief or hatred I have held towards myself or others, the faster and more successfully all my spells manifest.

GRIMOIRE EXERCISE
❋ *Working on Forgiveness* ❋

Take a time when the moon is waning as this will help with the energy of the drawing out of the poisons from the build-up of anger and betrayal that can be held in your body. I am not saying that anger is a bad energy. It is not, as it can be clean and clear, very powerful and useful. It is the force that when wedded with passion and a love of justice brings about great changes. It's what drives people to achieve the best in themselves. Anger at something that feels wrong or out of balance, combined with the love of something worthwhile, will bring about wonderful change. But combining anger with hatred and hurt can often lead to bitterness, and bitterness is like pouring poisoned water onto a plant, reading a book with the words all twisted up and tangled or acid rain pouring on the earth. It's not healthy, and we want healthy, powerful spellcasters. We want a clean, powerful, magickal you!

Let's do this work, knowing that we can stay active and fired up about justice but no longer holding on to festering anger that builds up resentment and hurt. This kind of anger does nothing to bring about a better life or, on a grander scale, a better planet.

GRIMOIRE EXERCISE

❋ *Clearing the Energy of Past* ❋
Unkindnesses in This Life or Others

All of us have thought or said or felt things we know we would rather not have at some time, and many of us have acted in ways that have been hurtful, foolish, selfish and unkind from time to time. We are human and we will do better from now on. However, sometimes there is a leftover energy from some of these acts, and it is worthwhile clearing the energy from these acts and finishing them for good. We can use this practice to forgive ourselves and to forgive others.

You'll need:
Your imagination, so you can visualise the person and the situation
You may wish to have some paper and a pen with you to take notes

What to do:
❋ Cast your circle.
❋ Call in the person you have hurt. Do not literally do this but do this in your mind's eye, using your amazing power of visualisation. This is very helpful if this is a person who you may never see again or if the person lives far away.
❋ Sit and speak with them. Do not justify your actions, but say whatever you need to say to them to let them know what led you to take the action you did.
❋ Ask for that person's forgiveness. It does not matter if it is unlikely they would forgive you in real life as you are working on an energetic level at the moment and working with that person's Higher Self. Really feel that forgiveness flow through you, freeing you.

✦ You must do this work for people who have hurt you. It can take time to forgive. It is also a very misunderstood process. Forgiveness is not about saying, 'Yes what you did was okay.' It may not have been okay – far from okay. But it is about forgiving that person so you can be free from the energy of the burning anger or hurt within you that weakens you and draws more of the same situation to yourself time and again. You won't forget, but now you must forgive too. You will be free.

CHAPTER 8

Working with Deities

You'll notice various spells ask you to call upon a God or a Goddess. For many people in our modern culture the word 'God' is loaded with meaning. Working with these deities is not like going to church and praying to a God who may or may not hear you. Calling upon these Gods and Goddesses, these Old Ones, is to draw from a deep well of powerful, primal energy.

Each deity has a unique and identifiable energy signature. Goddesses and Gods have symbols, animals that often appear with them, a time of day or night, or a phase of the moon during which they can be seen and connected with, and they have a very distinctive appearance. They may come to you in meditation, via visions and spontaneous intuitive flashes, in dreams, or throughout the natural world via the flowers, trees, animals and landscape.

Many people ask if these deities are real. Some magickal practitioners believe in Goddesses such as Artemis as a poetic truth, a kind of archetype, a way of personifying and understanding all that she represents. Others believe that she is very real and absolutely present. Many Witches call upon a deity when we wish to find that part of ourselves that mirrors the Divine and the qualities of that deity. This belief in the deity existing both externally and internally is a more modern view that sees us combining the reverence of our ancestors with the modern insights of transpersonal psychology. Whatever your beliefs, always remember that you need to approach deities with love, respect, dignity and reverence.

Working with deity can be a very humbling experience, as we open up to guidance and help from beyond our own self. It can be very powerful and connective – inspiring us to have courage and feeling protected and supported when we are more fragile, or when we are confronting a life test.

Be prepared to open your heart and turn your gaze to the world of deity, the energetic beings known by many as Gods and Goddesses. Here is a brief list of deities you might like to connect with. Always do some more research if you want to find out more about them.

Abundantia

This Roman Goddess of prosperity will help you grow a great crop of enriching energy and harvest it well. She will ensure your investments are fortunate and blessed.

Áine (pronounced ahn-neh)

This powerful and mysterious Irish Goddess has many forms, but she primarily works with light (moon and sunlight) and water. She will help you connect with your intuitive self and work with your psychic abilities in very practical and useful ways.

Amaterasu

The name of this graceful, caring Japanese Goddess means 'shining one in heaven', a mother figure who is much venerated and respected. She is a Sun Goddess who helps us lighten and brighten up and come out of sadness and darkness. She is also a weaver of sacred garments as an act of devotion.

Andraste

This ancient British Goddess of war can help resolve conflicts in your favour. Call her in to bring to you allies who have mutual interests. You are stronger when you do not fight alone.

Aphrodite

This Greek Goddess of love and sensuality promotes desire and sexual ecstasy and self-acceptance. She will help you with the ability to see beyond stereotypes in order to find your own unique expression of beauty and attractiveness.

Apollo

Apollo is the only God in the Greek pantheon powerful enough to pull the sun (which is the God Helios) across the sky in his sun chariot. He is also a keeper of promises — even if it brings him suffering. Approach him clearly and your outcome will shine bright.

Ares

Ares is a strong and active God of Ancient Greece who is very effective to call upon and work with if you are going to undergo a physical test, need extra energy or wish to hone your leadership skills. If you need his physical stamina please call on him, but be wary of his temper and bloodlust blinding you to what is really important in this challenge.

Arianrhod (pronounced are-ee-ahn-rod)

The Welsh Goddess Arianrhod will provide you with dreams and intuitive knowledge that can teach you the best way of coping with any kind of restrictions you may have. Even in the most powerless situation, and especially if it comes to issues of bullying and hurt, Arianrhod can help you find your strength and light your way forward.

Artemis

The Greek Goddess Artemis is excellent if you feel a little fuzzy around whether your intuition is clear enough for you to work with. She is young, vital, wild and fierce and is also a clean energy Goddess. Artemis is an amazing ally when it comes to a deity you can trust. She cares deeply for animals and young women.

Athena

Athena, the Goddess of war, justice and politics, is very, very strategic – she has armour and shielding and is very intelligent. She is a half-sister to Ares and her mother is Metis, a Goddess of careful, clear, thoughtful approaches and tests, a trait she has inherited.

Calling on a God or Goddess

*O*ne of the simplest and most beautiful ways of calling on a deity is simply to make a small offering and call their name. *Repetition of their name is actually magickal. Chanting the name of a God or Goddesses can place us in a space where we vibrate to the power of that energy being yet remain wholly ourselves.*

Build a relationship with them and call to them, either out loud or silently, from your heart. Feel confident in creating your own communications with the deities you wish to connect with. The energy you put into that will help strengthen the relationship greatly.

Bast

Bast, an Egyptian Goddess, is an agile, feline, sensual and independent Goddess unclouded by emotional thinking and is very regal. She is known as the 'Eye of the Night' and is associated with the moon. She is fiercely protective and territorial and is said to protect young women, especially at night. Bast can also disperse negativity and frighten off interlopers or invaders. She is most often depicted as a cat.

Baubo

If someone is grieving or very angry with you and stubborn, and is not speaking to you, call on this Greek Goddess to break through this wall of ice and laughter will bring you together again.

Boudicca

Boudicca was a queen of her people, the Iceni, who united the tribes of Britain and rose in revolt against Rome. Although she had many triumphs, she was captured and executed. Despite this, her valour and determination in the face of such odds has seen her become a venerated Goddess for many, symbolising courage, unity, justice and defiance.

Brigid

An ancient triple Goddess of Ireland, Brigid's worship was merged with that of Saint Brigid. She is a Goddess of poets, the forge, blacksmiths, animals, women, birth, new life, nursing and healing wells. Her maiden form is called Bride (Bry-dee or Bree) and her festival is Imbolc.

Cailleach

The Celtic Crone Goddess Cailleach often appears in the form she is most feared: a haggard, bone-thin old woman bringing winter to the landscape and death to the vulnerable. However, there is a gift in her harsh magick. She will save you much time and energy but it will mean some tough decisions. Her energy is strong, so appreciate this when you call on her.

Ceridwen

The Welsh Goddess Ceridwen is also known as a Witch and as a queen. She is a fiercely protective mother who concocts Awen, a magickal brew that endows the recipient with knowledge, language and long life. She is able to shapeshift into various forms and is a huntress. She inspires poets and, through challenging tests and initiations, she inspires us to become who we were always meant to be.

Cernunnos

Cernunnos, the Celtic Lord of the Wildwood, is also known as the 'Horned God' and is associated with stags, animals and the hunt. He is potent, fertile, lusty and powerful – a protector, provider and a consort to and lover of the Goddess Beltane.

Demeter

Demeter, the Mother Goddess of Greece, is the one directly associated with the turning of seasons and the growth of crops. She was the keeper of the mysteries of birth, life, death and afterlife, and great rites were held to honour her every solar cycle in Greece. We turn to her for warmth, growth, the revelation of secrets and to keep family connections strong and warm, even over long distances.

Diana

Diana, a mother and nurturer, is of great comfort and a reviver of health and power. She is associated with the full moon and is extremely healing.

Elen

The paleolithic British Goddess Elen is the keeper of the pathways and directions our soul can take in a lifetime. She helps us find our way when we are lost, guides us through transitions and provides us with all we need to survive in harsh times of change and challenge.

Eros

This Greek God of love Eros is powerful, almost intoxicating, in his energy, a strong, primal, masculine force. If you wish to feel the madness of love call on him, or if you wish him to lift the burden that such love and obsession can become ask him. His gift is not for all of us, for it is often impossible to bear and can create madness and pain as well as bliss and ecstasy.

Freya

This Nordic Goddess Freya is strong and has an energy that is supportive and inspiring. She literally inspires so much love that Viking warriors were willing to die for the possibility of being with her. Freya is beautiful, but she is also independent, strong and challenging. She is associated with the beautiful, potent energy of amber and its healing properties. Call on her to remain your own self and create respect within your relationship.

Ganesha

The elephant-headed Hindu God Ganesha can break through barriers with his strength. He is a gregarious God who loves helping humans. He is also a strong advocate of education and travel, and is known for his wisdom and brilliant, enduring memory. He helps us let go of people as well as helping you to grieve without falling prey to bitterness.

Hathor

The beautiful Egyptian Goddess Hathor can assist you to become more desirable, more confident and more attractive, and to become abundant and nurturing as well. Her tools include the mirror, and when you gaze at your reflection invoke her name to increase your natural beauty.

Hecate

Hecate is a Greek triple Goddess whose symbols are keys, the torch, a sacred flame and hounds. She is the keeper of the crossroads, and is able to cast light on which direction would be best for us to take in life. Her affinity with hounds symbolises her protective, guardian qualities, and her keys unlock the mysteries to dreams and to the Underworld. She has a symbol, called Hecate's Wheel, that can protect those who work with it and who call on her. She is often known as a dark Goddess and is treated with great respect.

Hermes

Look to the God Hermes when you need to find the right words and the right time to say them. He is extremely intelligent and very quick, so you will need to have your wits about you when you call on Hermes. If you wish to develop your telepathy, he is the one to call upon.

Hina

Hina is an Hawaiian butterfly Goddess who can help you speak truthfully, yet without becoming so emotional you cannot continue. Do call on Hina when you know you must have a conversation that is deep and emotional. She will help you express yourself from your heart without becoming overwhelmed.

Iris

Iris is often known as the beloved messenger of the dawn, and her powers have been revered since the time of Ancient Greece. She brings hope, a sense of understanding and awakening and optimism to hearts tired and worn. You will find your words have a powerful relieving effect, a calming and hopeful effect on others and on you, when you call on her.

Isis

Isis is the Egyptian Goddess of magick and is known as the Goddess of 10,000 faces. She is compassionate, warm and caring yet is so powerful she could bring Osiris, her husband, back from the dead. She cured the sun God Ra when he was ailing, and is the Goddess of medicine and of reading and of knowledge. She is perfect to call upon and consult with when you have been dealt a great blow by life – when you are wounded or torn apart by grief she can ease the pain and make you whole again.

Janus

Janus is the very earnest Roman God of beginnings and endings. He has two faces – one to face the past, the other to face the future – and he watches over the gateway threshold.

Jupiter

Energetically Jupiter is the Roman name for the God Zeus and you work with him to create good fortune and expansion. Working with him will also help you to develop as a person, grow mature and attract more power and abundance.

Kali

Kali is the Hindu Goddess of death and rebirth, and she is often depicted as dancing on bones, a bloodied knife in her hand and a necklace of skulls about her neck. This symbolises her ferocity – she will kill off the old in your life. Just know when you invoke her that there will be some destruction. She will also help protect you from any abusers, so definitely invoke her if you are being bothered or harassed or bullied and you want it to stop.

Kwan Yin

Kwan Yin is the Goddess of compassion and mercy. Her energy is exquisite
– gentle and warming, radiant and loving, profoundly caring and peaceful.
She can soothe troubled hearts and bring enlightenment and awareness to all
situations. She will help us all love without attachment or jealousy, and to
forgive without weakness or bitterness.

Lakshmi

I have a beautiful statue of Lakshmi in the front of my garden, and she is
depicted as very beautiful and tranquil. This Hindu Goddess brings abundance
and beauty into our lives, a feeling of satisfaction, completion and fullness.

Lugh

To work with Lugh, simply sit in the sunshine for a while and feel the light
on your face. Don't be afraid of the sun. One of the Celtic God Lugh's other
attributes is his talent at nearly everything he turns his clever hands to, so he
can help you multitask and be good at more than one thing at a time. He can
also help you approach difficult tasks with a certain lightness that can make
it less like a chore and more interesting and fun to work at.

The Morrighan

The Irish Goddess The Morrighan was said to beat on the shields of warriors
with her sword, roaring out a great battle speech to excite them into frenzy
before battle. She will create that sense of determination, an almost adrenalin
rush when you feel that you are confronted by a situation you cannot turn
away from. The Morrighan has a cloak of raven feathers, so do watch out for
black feathers – one of her signs that she is with you and offering support.

Odin

Call on Odin to write the correct words and communicate clearly. This Norse Father God is a very strong and decisive leader, adept at bringing disputes and conflicts to resolution. He is very old, very serious and has very solid energy. He also has great patience and is indisputably a leader, combining wisdom, communication skills and battle prowess.

Pele

Call on Pele, the Hawaiian Goddess of sensuality, dance and passion, to deal with guilt, temper, emotional inhibitions and lack of confidence. She is associated with volcanoes, the volcanic glass obsidian and the crystal peridot. She is fierce, dances, can walk on fire and she does not hold back.

Persephone

The Greek maiden Goddess Persephone is the daughter of the harvest Goddess, Demeter. Persephone is the herald of spring, flowers and newness. She is the bud, the potential and the life yet to be lived. She is the Goddess of maturation and of becoming independent from our parents, as well as finding freedom within close relationships.

Ra

Ra is the glorious Egyptian God of the sun. The Eye of Ra is the sun, the source of all life and power for humanity, and it is Ra who brings life, burning fiercely, seeing all.

Rhiannon

The Celtic Goddess Rhiannon teaches us about freedom, travel and self-determination. Her story involves escape from a tyrannical relationship and unjust punishment, and her independence and self-sufficiency from that time on. She takes lovers, is a mother and cares for people. She is associated with birdsong, horses, travel and independence.

Saturn

Saturn forces growing up on us and will not tolerate fun when there is something serious we need to face. He's a very stern task master, very earnest and humourless.

Sekhmet

The ferocious lioness-headed Goddess Sekhmet of Egypt has a strong relationship to Bast, but her power is tenfold. She is a huntress and her breath is so dry and hot it was said to have created the desert. She is the daughter of Ra and she can burn her enemies with her fiery gaze. She is implacable, a destroyer, and her weapon is fire, burning as hot as the surface of the sun. She is a warrior and a most fearsome enemy. Call upon her for protection and for courage.

Taliesin

Connect with the radiant Welsh deity Taliesin when you need to communicate with people or beings who are a little on the wild side. He has been given the gift of Awen, or divine inspiration, so he can inspire you to find the poetic way to express what you must say and connect with animals, birds, trees and nature. He speaks all languages and can assist you to learn other languages, or even just be understood.

Thor

Odin's athletic and impulsive son Thor possesses a hammer that can break through any obstacles before you — unsubtle as it may be. It can sometimes be necessary to take strong action when things are stuck and stagnant. He is greatly loved, and can restore life to those projects and creations that you once thought had no more vitality to them.

Thoth

Thoth is an Egyptian God whose powers include the gifts of the scribe — of writing, recording, history. He is intelligent and considered and a great diplomat. He has the head of the sacred ibis, and he developed language and the written word — or hieroglyphics, in the case of Egypt. He can help you connect with your urge to write or express yourself through language, and can be of assistance with contracts and legally binding papers and works. He is a mediator, and is also able to see through appearances and help you discover what is truly taking place in a situation.

Tyr

The often-forgotten Norse God Tyr's energy is moving back into the world. Tyr made enormous sacrifices to secure the future for his people, losing his right hand so a great destructive force in the world could be bound. This makes him a God to work with when you know doing something is going to have huge benefits not only for you but for others — and it may require a sacrifice and creative problem solving.

Valkyries

The Valkyries choose those who will be slain and taken to either Freya, in whose service they fight, or to Valhalla, presided over by Odin. They are the bringers of endings and also glory, and they only come to heroes. In many ways they can work with us to bring about an ending that must come. They are connected to ravens, to swans and to horses. To be in their presence is an ecstatic experience.

CHAPTER 9

Creating a Sacred Spellcasting Space

Have you ever walked into a room or entered someone's shop or even a park or garden and just felt a sense of comfort, rightness and inspiration? These spaces make you feel like you want to stay there a while. Then there are spaces that have nothing wrong with them at all but the energy feels off. This feeling can exist even when a room or space is filled with all the right spiritual stuff too – when the energy isn't working, no amount of crystals and purple velvet is going to fix this.

With this in mind, wherever you are going to do your spellwork needs to have that magickal, supportive, helpful and healthy vital energy. You need to feel great when you walk into the space. Having an outdoor space with the right energy that suits you is generally easy to find if you make sure it is safe and secluded enough for you to do your work, but some days it's going to be cold or raining or both and you're going to need a space indoors. Here are some easy and fun ideas to help you create a space that will make you feel magickal.

❊ MAKE YOUR SPACE PERSONAL ❊

Placement and space management is a magickal art that can be as simple as walking into a room and knowing that if you tidy up, clear the space and play different music, rearrange some objects and recharge what you love, everything will have a different energy. Adjust things in the space to suit you and you alone.

Creating a sacred spellcasting space is all about finding, creating and maintaining an environment in which you feel safe, comfortable, stimulated and peaceful and, most importantly, deeply connected. The space needs to be uplifting enough so that you don't feel so calm you sleep, nor so stimulating that you feel edgy and scattered. Many people are sensitive to the atmosphere of their space and will intuitively pick up on what is out of balance within an area. This intuition is something that comes naturally to magickal people. Always look after your sacred space. To me, energy shifting and working in a space is as routine as taking out the garbage and all that other stuff that we need to do. Doing magickal work creates debris and energetic leftovers, so make sure you work to clear this debris out of your magickal space and your life.

❋ WHEN TO CLEAR YOUR ❋ MAGICKAL SPACE

If you feel there is something not quite right in your space, clear it right away. If you are a planner and a practical person at heart, you could do it on a regular basis. It is a fantastic idea to get into a magickal 'housekeeping' routine. Here are some powerful times to do this magickal work.

- ❋ Use the waning moon to move energy out, especially strong energies that feel really glued in and very stuck.
- ❋ Use the new moon to bring beautiful new energies in. It is the best time for a blessing of a room or a house.
- ❋ A full moon is a powerful amplifier of energies. For me, I tend to clear a little before working with full moon energy as it is so strong. I am more inclined to do my magickal workings during a full moon rather than clear and bring in during it.

❋ THE RIPPLE EFFECT ❋

Whatever you do in your magickal space is going to have an impact on everyone around you — remember the law of the threefold return? (See page 9.) It will send out a kind of ripple effect that will be felt in many other areas. This ripple effect will be a little more contained in your magickal space, but it's a kind of energetic bath for your space that renews, invigorates and maintains the mental, physical and spiritual health of everyone within your home or wherever you've chosen to create your space. It also increases the wonderful experiences, people and prosperity drawn to you.

A space can simply be imbued with energetic debris of past occupants and incidents, and the energy with which the room or home was created can certainly be felt many years after the original work has been done. The land on which a space is built will also bring its influence to bear on the atmosphere of a home. Essentially, many dilemmas or problems for occupants can be solved in peaceful, loving ways that have spiritual integrity at their core.

There can be rooms in which you feel extremely light-headed and faint in certain areas. You may also notice that in some rooms, homes, even suburbs, it's the people who live there who create the energy imbalances. If people are very unhappy or have lived lives in which they have had big problems to overcome or are ill or bitter or just plain nasty, their energy can leak outwards, hanging like an energetic cloud. Regardless of the source of the energy, clearing, cleansing and rebalancing works.

It's also a great idea to have a cleansing and energy clearing when you move into a new home. This is an important part of establishing your space as your own. The energy in a space does not need to be banished, but it needs to hold and emanate the essence of your personal energy, otherwise it may continue supporting the wishes and intentions of people who are no longer present.

White Candle Space-clearing Spell

Enter the space you wish to clear. Be sure you can be alone for about 20 minutes. This spell works best with as few external influences about as possible.

You'll need:
A white candle
Some salt for sprinkling
Blessed water

What to do:

❋ Take the white candle and sprinkle the salt around it in a widdershins direction. This is for clearing and banishing.

❋ Light the candle and let it burn down. As it does, know its flame is burning through all energetic debris and leaving your space clear, calm and bright with potential.

❋ When the candle has burned down, collect the wax and salt and bury them in the ground. Sprinkle more salt and blessed water over where it is buried to keep the energy safe and transmuting below the ground.

❋ How to Make a Smudge Stick ❋

This is an old magickal practice that exists all over the planet, so when you work with smoke and clearing you are joining a long line of magickal practitioners in shifting and moving and transmuting unhealthy energy.

You'll need:

Fresh herbs. You can choose from any kind, but they need to be fresh and in lengths, not pre-dried and pre-cut. These are readily available. Of course, it is always best if you grow your own. All herbs have different qualities:

BASIL is a herb that creates a great environment for students, strong memory and clear thinking.
GRANDFATHER SAGE is a powerful and traditional clearer of negative energy.
LAVENDER soothes and calms and creates a nurturing, wise space. Wonderful to use if there are sleep disturbances.
MARJORAM is enriching and invigorating. Marjoram increases your ability to think clearly.
ROSEMARY helps to clear, but also reinforces positive memories and helps you make wise choices.
THYME is a herb associated with faery energy and wellness and has a lively, revitalising energy.

❋ Dry the herbs by hanging lengths of them in a space that is moisture free and well ventilated. It's lovely and is a beautiful energy boost too. Wrap string or ribbon around the ends of the herbs, knot it three times, leave a little bit of length in the string and tie the herbs so they hang upside down.

* After three days, take down your herbs and wrap them tightly at the base and slightly looser along the length with a pure thread such as cotton or silk.
* Carefully light the end, and then staunch it so there's no flame, just smoke. Always have some water handy in case a spark lands somewhere!
* Walk through the house or sacred space widdershins holding your smudge stick, fanning the smoke out into the space before you. Pay particular attention to areas where the energy feels stuck or unpleasant.
* You need not burn the whole smudge stick down — just use enough so that you have smoked out the unpleasant energy.

CHAPTER 10

Seven Spells in Seven Days

If you really want to create a magickal new life, the results you get are going to be directly associated with the effort you put in and the steps you take to action your magick. If you work your magick with all your heart and soul, backing up your spells with commitment and energy, they'll work. Life will change its shape. Remember the word 'wicce' and how it holds the bending and weaving of energy? If you are witchcrafting you are bending and weaving the energy, that raw material the Universe has been so generous to bless you with. When you become a spellcaster you become an energy sculptor, and that raw energy will be shaped strongly by spellwork that is clean, intuitive, determined, disciplined, yet relaxed and fun.

To get started on this process, here is a magickal guide to casting one life-changing spell a day for seven days to give you a very powerful week. This is a great way to learn about the energies of each of the days of the week while practising your spellcasting. You see, every single day in this pattern we've formed called a calendar holds a lot of energy, and each day's energy is different, holding unique potential for us to work with.

For these seven days and seven spells to really change your life you need to bring some power and energy to this, so get enthused and committed. Remember why you're doing this work. Remind yourself of this when you get a little lazy and feel that you can just coast by on your natural gifts and the natural energy around you.

One sound way to maintain your commitment is to know that sometimes your plan is going to go wrong and you need to let yourself know that this is okay. Simply refocus and keep going on the seven-day challenge. This exercise is about creating a new life via your new commitments.

You have to put the energy in. And remember it is not all hard work – it's going to be a lot of fun and you're going to have a really amazing time gathering and growing these new skills.

After you've spellcast, record your observations and feelings in your Grimoire every day, every night.

❋ MONDAY: EMOWER YOUR INTUITION ❋

Monday is one of the most magickal days of the week – it's a great day to start, but it can be challenging. This is because Monday means 'moon day' so it contains and holds all the energies of beautiful, powerful Luna. This is the day when everything that is underneath can rise up: it is a day for secrets, to be kept or to be revealed. It's also a day for psychic moments. Intuitive hunches and imaginings all can become very clear and demand your attention. It is a great day to dream up ideas, to make progress on working with your intuition, to get in touch with your femininity and celebrate the Goddess within. A kind of serenity is Monday's gift.

Today's spiritual assignment is to get back in touch with the creative, imaginative side.

Note what phase the moon is in and gaze upon its form in the evening. Moonlight is an essential ingredient in our makeup and it is beneficial for our health to spend time under moonlight, as it also reconnects us to the natural world and to our imaginations. Wear something silver or metallic pastels to help you channel that lunar energy all day long.

Monday Meditation

This meditation will only take five minutes. Dress in loose white clothing and sit comfortably on the floor or in a chair. Rest your hands on your knees with your palms facing upwards. Touch your index finger to your thumb, as this will keep your energy directed within. Allow yourself to simply breathe and sit and be. Allow your thoughts to happen, but do not indulge them or activate them. After meditating, run yourself a warm sea salt or Epsom salts bath to complete your spiritual awakening with a beautiful cleansing that will drain away negativity. Pat yourself dry with a big fluffy towel and moisturise your skin.

Monday Moon Spell

Here is a beautiful spell to connect more powerfully with your intuition and psychic guidance. It can help make sense of dreams and flashes of insight, and help you know what to do with this dream energy.

You'll need:
A silver or pale blue pencil for drawing on skin (eyeliner is perfect)
A moonstone

What to do:
❈   Cast a circle, and say three times:

Artemis, clear my sight
Under moonlight, oh, so bright
Artemis, hear my call
Release me from whatever thrall.

Endow me with the magickal power
To bring me back from confusion's hour
Make my sight clear and true
I allow myself to be guided by you.

❈   Draw a crescent or sickle moon on your brow.
❈   Lie down. Place the moonstone on your forehead.
❈   Feel the energy of the moon and your insight returning.
❈   Call your insight back, really bringing your focus and intention to seeing energy and insight returning. Feel your intuition becoming unblocked. Feel the sense of being empowered.

- ❀ Release the bonds of believing that your intuition is wrong or stupid or foolish.
- ❀ Release the belief that you are making things up and know that you are powerfully intuitive. When this intuition is married with the clear direction of Artemis' bow you will be clear, bright and softly determined, just as the moon is.
- ❀ Ask for any insights you may find useful at this time to come to you now. Write these down in your Grimoire.
- ❀ Close your circle, and place your moonstone in your sacred space. Write in your Grimoire the impact your spellcasting had on you immediately.
- ❀ Have a wonderful rest. Let your dreams speak to you of tomorrow.

Monday Magick at a Glance

RULING PLANET: the moon (technically a celestial body, not a planet) represents femininity, imagination and intuition.

MAGICKAL STONES: rock crystal, moonstone, pearl, any white, milky stone.

ON THIS DAY WEAR: feminine flowing garments to reactivate your lunar energies. Choose the colours of white, silver, grey and metallic pastels.

AFFIRMATION: 'I am in touch with my intuition and I listen to my divine guidance.'

ESSENTIAL OILS: sandalwood for protection, jasmine for sensuality.

ACTION: explore intuition, dreams and psychic talents. A great day to purchase a deck of tarot or oracle cards and begin to explore using them

ENERGY: dreamy, world between worlds. It's wonderful, if you can, to maintain this dreamy quality all day long.

DEITIES: Selene, Aine, Artemis, Diana, Arianrhod.

❋ Tuesday: Activate Your Energy ❋

Tuesday is a day of inspired action. It's also potentially a day of confrontation and battles — of challenges and tests of your courage and determination. It is considered to be a masculine day, but it's limiting to label this energy by gender as there is plenty of female warrior energy in this world. You can tap into this today, which gives you a brilliant chance to tackle anything that has been frightening or challenging you, such as a conversation you need to have, a bully you need to stand up to, a fight you need to engage in. It is a day of fire and energy and power, and your levels of intensity will go up today. To best work with and harness this energy you need to keep it contained and under control but not tight and compressed, and remember that sometimes a certain lightness accompanied by a lot of action and determination will help you do brilliantly. It is also a great day to compete and physically push yourself. Physical exertion will help calm you as the energy is quite volatile this day.

Tuesday Meditation

What does the Universe want you to know about courage? Write down the thoughts you have regarding your own power, good or bad, and begin to reconnect with your ability to create your own life regardless of who seems to stand in your way.

The Courage of Tyr spell for Tuesday

YOU'LL NEED:

A river rock or flat stone (one larger than a 20 cent coin is best)

Some red paint and a fine paintbrush

A black candle

A red candle

A small black bag or pouch

WHAT TO DO:

* ❋ At dawn or dusk, open your circle.
* ❋ Take your river rock and, using the red paint and brush, inscribe the rune for Tyr.
* ❋ On your black candle, write what it is you are fearful of, what makes you feel small.
* ❋ Identify the situation or the person confronting you.
* ❋ On the red candle, write your name, Tyr's symbol and the times in life you have shown great courage. Say now:

Great Tyr

Who held back Ragnarok and the great wolf Fenris with the sacrifice of your hand

Lend to me now your courage to face what must be faced

For if you could face this loss and sacrifice for the greater good of all

Then so can I, even though I feel so small.

* ❋ Light the black candle, and as it burns know too the fears and worry are melting away. Bury the wax and say:

You have no power over me, fears. I am strong and brave.
I know the way of Tyr.

❋ Light the red candle. As it burns, feel it filling you with its flame of courage. Understand you will have tests to face, but like Tyr you will come away from these knowing you have defeated a great threat. There will be a sacrifice – of your time, of your comfort perhaps and definitely of your habits and belief about yourself – but know Tyr has made the greatest sacrifice of all in holding back the wolf of Ragnarok so we can live. You need have no fear, for if he could do this what is it in comparison that you fear? You can do this as the God Tyr has your back literally and is giving you the space and courage to go ahead with what must be done.

❋ Thank Tyr for his sacrifice, telling him you are inspired by his courage and that you will not let him or the other heroes down.

❋ See yourself with a winged helmet and a shield and filled with courage.

❋ Keep the circle open until you do what must be done.

❋ Close your circle, and keep the river rock and the red candle wax in the black bag until you require the assistance of this brave God.

Tuesday Magick at a Glance

RULING PLANET: Mars.

MAGICKAL STONES: garnet, carnelian, ruby, firestone and obsidian.

ON THIS DAY WEAR: reds and the colours of flame – for energy, passion, courage.

AFFIRMATION: 'I love being brave. I am filled with courage.'

ESSENTIAL OIL: ylang ylang, which is revitalising and sensual, also alleviates headaches and de-stresses when energy levels become way too high, as they can do on a Tuesday.

ACTION: find a way to energise your body every week that you love such as martial arts, boxing classes and physical challenges that will awaken your energy and power. Learn the haka!

ENERGY: very active, the one day each week when you really can extend yourself physically and get the very best results.

DEITIES: Tyr, Boudicca, The Morrighan, Ares.

✳ Wednesday: Let's Connect ✳ and Understand

Wednesday has quite a few influences and it's a complex day in lots of ways. While it is about communication and comprehension and understanding and that deep connection we can have, it can also be about deep conversations, resolutions and the time we take to communicate well. It is associated with Odin, the great father God of the Norse pantheon, so take what is said and communicated very seriously. Odin was also about sacrificing something in order to be able to communicate in a new way, so perhaps a perspective can be sacrificed on a Wednesday and the reward will be insightful, wise communication and respect for your efforts. This is also a great day to write a letter, a blog, an essay: anything to do with words is going to be supported. You can have a great chat and you can also sign and write songs and play music better – or be inspired by this musical energy to this day! Wednesday's energy is also really intellectual – you can do some beautiful, bright thinking.

Wednesday Meditation

Meditate on the way you communicate and ask your Higher Self (the part of you that is directly connected to what we call Source or the Universe or God/Goddess) what it is you need to learn about communicating. Focus on communicating that creates healthy relationships. Visualise healthy conversations, even about difficult topics, and affirm to yourself: 'I now find the right words for every situation. Listening is empowering. Everyone benefits when I speak from my heart.'

The Naming Spell

Often in life our name is said with anger or criticism and over time we begin to take on that energy, especially when we are young and at a vulnerable point in our life. This spell or ritual can undo this damage. It can be done alone or with one or more others.

WHAT TO DO:

✷ Take yourself to your altar and sit quietly for a moment. If you are on your own, call in guides and loved ones or friends. Imagine that your family members from whom you crave approval are there.

✷ Begin to hear them saying your name, over and over, with love, and say your name to yourself as well, with love, tenderness, pride and infuse into your name all the energy you would wish it to be said with. Your name will soon begin to sound and feel quite different. If you are doing this with actual friends, you might enter into a state of slight trance. You will know when enough is enough as the energy will naturally peak, then gently fall, and integrate within you. Your name has been 'changed'. You may wish to say your name again and again to yourself in ways that are beautiful, admiring, caring, encouraging and positive. Watch this magick undo all the negativity you have carried. You don't need to do this spell all the time but do use it when there is hostility and even abuse around you. In more extreme cases you can do this spell and change your name. Be wary, though, that if you change your name too often you will lose some credibility in your work.

Wednesday Magick at a Glance

RULING PLANET: Mercury.

MAGICKAL STONES: turquoise, lapis lazuli, blue sapphire.

ON THIS DAY WEAR: blue for harmony, communication and clarity.

AFFIRMATION: 'I enjoy expressing my ideas and beliefs.'

ESSENTIAL OILS: lime and orange blends spice up conversations and get people chatting easily. These oils are ideal for communication.

ACTION: talk to like-minded souls about what you believe and where you're going. Wednesday is an auspicious day to put it out there, to express out loud your dreams and wishes. It is also a fabulous time to join a group or engage in therapy, maybe even get involved in an online forum.

ENERGY: intellectual, witty, interactive. Wednesday is a constructive day for working in a group and finding the support we all need for our journey.

DEITIES: Hermes, Baubo, Odin, Taliesin, Iris, Hina.

❋ Thursday: Create Abundance ❋

Money is just one of the forms energy takes. People create wealth and money out of energy they attract, generate — or even inherit, then the money itself can be translated into lots of other energies and empower projects and plans. Magickal people have often been notoriously ineffective at handling finances! That's because there are still to this day so many people who will claim you must NEVER accept money for your magickal work.

Sometimes there's a feeling that we don't deserve money and prosperity — that there is something horrid about money or being materialistic. Why do we think this? Well, we get so many double messages about money and prosperity it results in a great deal of desire for money, and an even greater deal of guilt and resentment around having it! This means that while we wish to have money we fear having it, fearing that it will make us nasty, unliked, perhaps a target for envy and jealousy. Today is your day to bring this relationship back into balance, or to work at getting an after-school job, earning your own money or coming up with clever ideas.

Thursday Meditation

Find a quiet, private place. Clear your mind, ground and settle. Take three deep breaths and affirm eight times out loud: 'I am connected to the source of all prosperity.'

Pause, wait, feel the truth of this settling in your body.

Clear your mind. Reground and settle. Take three deep breaths. Take your time.

Affirm eight times: 'All my needs are already taken care of.'

If you wish, keep the affirmations going. Be sure to repeat them in cycles of eight. When you feel the truth of your words radiating out from you, you will know the work is done.

Lakshmi Abundance Chant

❀ Open your circle. You may make a border of flowers and blessed water, and a little salt for a little extra magick.

❀ Take a deep breath, then sing or chant 108 times one of Lakshmi's two great mantras 'Shreem brzee' or 'Om brzee namaha.' As you do so visualise gold and abundance shining from you, radiating out. Traditionally beads were strung to keep count of your chants and to know when you have finished each cycle. You may wish to do this or you can offer Lakshmi rose petals or small flowers each time you sing the mantra. Keep your heart open and expansive, and feel her compassion and bounty pouring like liquid energetic gold into your every cell. Glow with her blessings!

❀ Imagine all the good you will do when you have enough money to spend in different ways. Imagine spending money on causes you wish to support and people whose creativity you want to support. Imagine the comfort and the generosity, the power and support and freedom. Thank her now, with all your heart. Support your chanting with your belief.

❀ After you have completed the mantras, as an offering to Lakshmi sweep your front and back steps so her bounty can flow through and reach you. Always sweep your floor and your doorway and keep it clean and clear, and sprinkle a little essential oil blend about these areas (see the recipe opposite). They are the sentinels to your abundance and your willingness to receive it. Keep them clear and receptive, so abundance from Goddess Lakshmi can flow through to you.

❀ When you are finished, close your circle in your usual and your own way.

Lakshmi's Abundance Oil

This blend is soothing, loving and invigorating. Bless and anoint yourself with this oil before doing your work, and once each waxing moon do your Lakshmi devotions.

Three drops of grapefruit oil
A drop of patchouli oil
A drop or two of rose oil, or a rose variation of your choice
(rose maroc or rose otto, for example)
A drop or two of jasmine oil
A few drops of lime oil

Thursday Magick at a Glance

RULING PLANET: Jupiter.

MAGICKAL STONES: stone, smoky quartz.

ON THIS DAY WEAR: earthy tones, as these colours will reconnect you to the earth's growth energy and give you a solid feeling from which to face challenges.

AFFIRMATION: 'It is safe for me to manifest my abundance.'

ESSENTIAL OILS: basil for clear, practical thinking and focus — being spiritual also means being connected — and on a Thursday evening have a bath with seven drops of bergamot to uplift your energy, clear debt and attract prosperity.

ACTION: examine your attitudes to money and prosperity.

ENERGY: you can make large, bold changes regarding your beliefs on a Thursday.

DEITIES: Lakshmi, Jupiter, Thor, Ganesha, Abundantia.

✳ FRIDAY: LOVE, ATTRACTION ✳ AND BEAUTY

Friday is a day that is named for the Nordic Goddess Freya, who was not only a Goddess who inspired passionate love and deep devotion, she was a guardian and lover of warriors too.

So the question with Friday is what is going on with your relationships? How do you feel about yourself and your ability to attract a beautiful, fulfilling and fun relationship into your life?

It's time for you to take back control of how you feel about your physicality, your sensuality and your own attractiveness. You have that real, deep life spark within you, a flame, and any negativity around love can be really helped and healed on a Friday. Freya, who is a very kick-arse Goddess, will show you the way.

Friday Meditation

Today, work with a crystal associated with love. Rose quartz, garnet or ruby would be suitable, as would amber, Freya's stone. Sit quietly, holding your crystal in your non-dominant hand. In your mind's eye, see a beautiful love heart beginning to form. See it change shape and colour and keep bringing it back to health. Examine it closely: if you see any energetic debris – any thorns, swords, pieces of wire, cuts or bruises or tangled cords – gently see them dissolving in your mind's eye. When you have done this cleansing work take your crystal, hold it to your heart and say: 'My heart is loving and unhurt.'

Let the energy subside. Collect yourself, eat something sweet to ground you and go about your Friday.

Freya's Strength in Love Spell

This is a wonderful all-round spell where you will be working with a Goddess who is powerful, war-like, fiercely independent and extremely intelligent. Is it any wonder that Viking warriors called out her name on the battlefield? She is associated with amber and cats so we'll be using both these elements to connect with her.

The love you draw with this spell is very empowering and is wonderful to cast to really connect with all the different aspects of you – the emotional side who weeps, or the one who isn't ready to back down from a confrontation. This is especially good for fiery men and women who wish to work with a Goddess who understands their temper!

YOU'LL NEED:

A beeswax candle

Some amber essential oil or perfume

A little gold dust (gold dust is often sold as a cosmetic;

if it is difficult to find, substitute gold glitter)

A gold cloth for preparing your altar

Some cat fur, preferably from a black or golden cat

but don't stress too much about this

A mirror

WHAT TO DO:

❋ Open your circle and say:

Freya, Golden One, I call to thee

I offer to you this amber and gold

I ask for your help

For your wisdom so bold.
I ask now for courage
For truth and to shine
I ask for your power, your strength so divine
I call now for love, but one that will be
A strong growing oak, a king among trees
Make my love a clean river that flows to the sea
Make my love an offering to be proud of, for thee.

❁ Repeat this three times or more and as you do, take the candle and roll it in some amber essential oil or anoint the candle with a little amber perfume. (This is amber from tree resin, not ambergris from whales! Amber essential oil is readily available online.)

❁ Sprinkle it in gold dust and carve the three runic symbols into it.

Berkano   Gebo   Mannaz

❁ On your altar, place the gold cloth and cat fur, sprinkle some more gold dust and place your amber candle. Put the mirror on the altar so that you can look at yourself.

❁ Light the candle on your golden altar. By candlelight, look into your face and see it merge with Freya's and feel beautiful, strong, wise and nurturing, fiercely protective, so attractive and inspiring.

❁ If Freya has any wisdom to offer you, write this down in your Grimoire.

❁ Close your circle. Give thanks.

Note: keep a close eye out for butterflies or cats, either actual or symbolic, as they are signs that Freya is with you and has answered your call.

Friday Magick at a Glance

RULING PLANET: Venus.

MAGICKAL STONES: rose quartz, ruby, sapphire, amber, garnet.

ON THIS DAY WEAR: pink, rose, red and gold tones as this is your day for expressing your inner love Goddess.

AFFIRMATION: 'I am worth loving, exactly as I am.'

ESSENTIAL OILS: rose absolute, amber perfume.

ACTION: tell someone you love them. And tell yourself, too.

ENERGY: sensual, playful, flirtatious, strong, open, receptive.

DEITIES: Freya, Hathor, Rhiannon, Eros, Aphrodite.

✳ Saturday: the Big Picture ✳

Saturday is a day for things to be taken seriously and to think your future through. It's a day to get rid of what you don't want. This is a day with a big kick to it, making it a very good day for deciding what you do not want to take place in your life anymore. The planet Saturn is famous for getting us to grow up, giving us the lesson we need to get through a particularly challenging time or moment. This is a day when a lot of things come to an end, including some friendships, behaviours and habits. If you have aspects of your personality that you are not too impressed with, this is a great day for saying to yourself you are going to get rid of them.

Saturday Meditation

For this meditation, as always, find yourself a quiet, private place. Light a candle. Stare into its flame, and bring your attention to your breath. Slowly now – in and out, in and out. When you are calm and centred, repeat over and over: 'It is safe for me to let go. I surrender control of the outcome to the my Higher Self and to the Universe.'

Repeat five times (for change) and continue to say this in cycles of five until you feel you have moved some of the energy.

Go about your Saturday ready to let go and face necessary endings in order to bring about change.

The Witch's Broom Spell

Witches' broomsticks, also known as besoms, are magickal tools that cleanse, clear and dislodge old, stuck energy. With this spell, watch the profound energetic difference that working with your Witch's broom can make.

YOU'LL NEED:
9 sprigs of rosemary
9 sprigs of sage
3 small leafy twigs of eucalypt, tea tree or pine (very sturdy trees)
A 30-cm piece of strong black cord or string
A handful of sea salt for sprinkling on the floor
Black candle wax (optional)
A piece of onyx (optional)
Some sandalwood

WHAT TO DO:
* ❋ Cast your circle.
* ❋ Bind the herbs and leafy twigs with the cord, wrapping it around the base of the bunch nine times (or multiples of nine if your cord is longer). Tie five knots at the end of the cord. As you do this, say:

I sweep you from me, I let you go
Whether you are friend or foe
If you are not meant to be with me
I release you, see, I set you free
You cannot return, even if you would
Unless you be for my highest good
Thus with my spell, I set thee free
As I do will, so mote it be.

❋ You can just use this besom or broom if you wish or you can sprinkle salt around your floor to increase the cleaning energy. Leave it there for a while and let the salt absorb any unwanted energy. As you sprinkle the salt say:

Salt, salt, cast about
Soak it up, we live without
The old and the stale, the unwanted word
The deed, the feeling, the cruelty heard
Soak it up
I'll cast it out
We shall be free
There is no doubt.

❋ Sweep your home with your broom in a widdershins direction – clockwise southern hemisphere, anti-clockwise northern hemisphere. Remember, this is the banishing direction. You are sweeping your space free of tension, aggression, malice, jealousy, spite, envy and cruelty, even when expressed from someone you love. If you wish you can attach a larger branch to your sweeper to make a bigger broom and seal it with black candle wax and glue, and fix a piece of onyx or black tourmaline or obsidian to your broom, perhaps again with beeswax or a natural, low-toxin craft glue. This will give your Witch's broom the power to create a protective barrier in all the places you have cleansed.

❋ After you have done this, vacuum up every trace of the salt.

❋ Burn sandalwood and feel the new peace bloom in your space.

❋ Put your Witch's broom away until you next need her magick.

❋ Close your circle and thank all who have helped you this day.

Saturday Magick at a Glance

RULING PLANET: Saturn.

MAGICKAL STONES: smoky quartz, slate, black onyx, obsidian.

ON THIS DAY WEAR: something that makes you feel more serious, determined, very clear in your intention. For many people black works well. It represents a funeral for the habits you're letting go of.

AFFIRMATION: 'It is safe to change. I am now moving into a wonderful new stage of my life.'

ESSENTIAL OILS: frankincense, sandalwood, sage.

ACTION: releasing what holds you back within yourself. This is not a day to blame other people for how things are. You have to take responsibility! Write down one habit or behaviour you know you could get rid of.

ENERGY: committed, final and ready to make big decisions about what needs to go in order to create the future you desire.

DEITIES: Kali, Valkyries, Janus, Saturn, Cailleach, Cerridwen.

☀ Sunday: Rebirth and Joy ☀

Sunday is a beautiful day. It is a day to praise and give yourself over to the happiness of a higher power – which in my case is natural magick, the world of the trees and the sky and the energy flows. It is a day to go to the church of your soul, which might be the beach, where you find yourself inspired by the power of the waves and the courage and skill of surfers, or you might want to listen to music you love, make an amazing playlist, hang out with friends or family who inspire, support and enjoy you and do something fun and exciting together. It is not about taking risks or defying authority. Ultimately, Sunday is about setting up your week so you shine each day – relighting your own internal flame so you can go into the world bright and strong, attractive and protected. The glow and flame you ignite today will burn bright all week.

Sunday Meditation

Your meditation today is active and moving. You are going to create a beautiful altar celebrating light and radiance. You can freestyle this, but here are some suggestions for magickal items you may wish to include:

* gold stones, such a citrine, tiger's eye, amber
* gold dust or glitter
* golden cloth
* bright yellow flowers such as marigolds, sunflowers or daffodils.

Create a beautiful arrangement with your objects. If you have a deck of tarot cards you may wish to place the Sun card on your altar. Its energy will bring good cheer and positive vibes to your home all day long and into the week ahead.

Brigid's Flame Spell

Sunday is a day of beauty and initiation. This day we ask Brigid to relight your fire within. What you bring to this day will ripple out into time and space, creating tomorrow after tomorrow. Think well and hard on dreams and what it is you wish to create with your life.

YOU'LL NEED:
A blue cloth for your altar
1 beeswax candle and a candlestick
Sweet orange oil
A small quantity of gold dust or glitter
A sharp stick or pencil to carve into the candle

WHAT TO DO:
* Cast a circle.
* Set up your altar with the blue cloth and anoint the beeswax candle with the oil. As you do say:

Sweet Brigid, my mother, light from the ashes of my spirit
An undying flame
Light within my deepest parts
Your fire, your spark
Reignite my heart
Until the brightness that's mine
Flows from me and shines
Out into the world
In word and in deed
Of your flame, of your fire
I shall always have need.

❊ Sprinkle around the candle the gold dust, and from this spread nine rays of light in glitter. Say:

Nine rays, three rays, of imbas, the three drops of knowledge
and of holy light.

❊ Light your candle and say:

As I light this candle
So my fire is rekindled by Brigid
A flame eternal
To inspire, heal, comfort and warm me.

❊ Place the candle in a candlestick and hold your hands just above the flame, feeling the heat. Scoop the heat from the flame up in your hands and hold it over your heart. You will feel Brigid's love warming you. Repeat, but this time hold the heat over your lips so that your words be warm and true.

❊ Look deep into the flame of Brigid and know this is a healing flame, one that will bring peace, harmony, compassion, courage and wit to any time and place. Remind yourself that Brigid is your mother and will care for you. You are within her forge when you light this candle. You are creative and caring and independent and reborn each time this candle is lit.

❊ Thank Brigid and write down in your Grimoire any messages or feelings or thoughts you may have had.

❊ Think for a moment and resolve to have courage and to burn brightly and steadily, like her flame, and forge a great life as her forge creates over and over again.

❊ Blow out the flame, sending wishes into the week as you do so.

❊ Wait till the wax is cool, then roll the candle in more gold dust. Carve a Brigid's cross upon the candle. Use this candle to light other candles each time you cast this spell.

❊ Close your circle and enjoy a deep, peaceful sleep.

Sunday Magick at a Glance

RULING PLANET: the sun.

MAGICKAL STONE: citrine.

ON THIS DAY WEAR: gold, yellow, orange for good cheer and to attract positive people to you.

AFFIRMATION: 'I am a star. I shine. I have enough light for myself and for others. I am warm and powerful.'

ESSENTIAL OILS: sandalwood, sweet orange, neroli, lime, oak moss.

ACTION: build an altar in the morning and host a gathering to celebrate the new you in the afternoon.

ENERGY: the sun's energy on Sunday helps us walk our talk and be more who we are, comfortable in our skin, and allows us to radiate success without feeling uncomfortable. This is the day to begin to shine for yourself and for others.

DEITIES: Apollo, Amaterasu, Lugh, Brigid.

When you have completed this week, be very proud of yourself. Your dedication, commitment and energy, along with your intention, are already making magickal waves in your life. Well done, spellcaster. Thou art magick.

Chapter 11

Love
Spells

They are innocent-looking words, aren't they: love spells? Do not be fooled: this is powerful magick! I remember well the first time I deliberately cast a love spell. Oh, learn from me, I made so many mistakes. I thought I knew better than the Universe. I was in the thrall of one of those crushes — a burning, 24 hours in the day obsessive crush. I knew I wanted him and so I cast, using his photo and focusing on him, him and him. Usher in mistakes two, three, four. So funny how things work out. I learned this lesson not once, but twice. One time I didn't even cast, but I worked with all my powers, my energy, my intention to make what I thought I wanted. A great big painful, messy lesson! In short, when we cast for love we have to, in some ways, leave the outcome to the Goddess and the God (the feminine and masculine divine) and get out of our own way. We do not cast for a person and we do not try to take someone we want from another, because this is an area where that threefold law really comes into play, undeniably.

I know this too, because one out of every two questions I am asked as a Witch is 'Can you cast a love spell for me?' Spells are times when we put aside a moment to practise loving . . .with every stitch of our charm pouch or use of rose petal, love stirs, awakens and grows within, and we send out that energy and draw it towards us.

So, to minimise backfiring these spells are absolutely safe and loving yet they are very serious in their intent. It's a good and worthy goal — to help bring more love into your life. Remember that when working love magick, free will is of the greatest importance. We do not cast to draw a specific person.

Some of these spells are going to require more work. Others are simpler, less time consuming. You will know which to do.

And, so, this is where we begin.

Self-love spell

This spell will help you break through barriers, eliminating negative thought patterns you've held on to about yourself. Do this with all of your heart and watch the changes begin.

YOU'LL NEED:

A private space and some alone time for at least an hour

A large mirror

Clay (you can purchase really gorgeous refined white and pink clays, or you can get very earthy about this and collect your own clay)

A beautiful red piece of cloth

A picture of yourself that you like — better still, one you love

A little bit of your hair

A candle

WHAT TO DO:

* Open your circle. Once you've cast your circle, take off your clothes. Standing skyclad before the mirror, really see your body. Allow yourself to see the beauty and perfection of all that you are, no matter how imperfect you may judge yourself to be.

* Take the clay and cover the part of your body you have negative or critical thoughts about. Clay draws out impurities so really feel it drawing out of you all criticisms, all negative thoughts, all the physical negativity that may have held you back from being healthy and comfortable, loving and accepting about your own body.

* When you feel the energy reach a peak, take yourself to the shower, turn on the water hard and really know that along with the clay running down the drain so too are all the old fears and doubts

and self-criticisms. They're history! You are worthy of love, self-love, the love of others. You deserve respect. Stand tall, as tall as you can under the water. Let this belief flow right into you.

* Step out of the shower and dry yourself off with a beautiful soft towel.
* Go back to your room or sacred space.
* Take your red cloth and make a little altar. Place on this your picture of yourself, and around this place your hair. If you have short hair that's okay; just pop a little about. Light a candle on the altar.
* To the picture of yourself, and to you, say out loud:

I love my body, it is beautiful and strong
I love my mind, it's clear and clever
I love my spirit, it's bright and high
I love my feelings, they're human and heartfelt
I love myself exactly as I am right now.

* Close your circle. Snuff out the candle. Shake yourself a little, put on some music that is uplifting and eat something sweet to ground you. For the next seven days put a little clay on whatever part of your body you feel critical about. Within one lunar cycle you'll be more grounded in your self-love. You will believe you are beautiful and worthy of love, and you will shine.

Make a Magickal Love Charm

This charm pouch will gently, safely yet strongly attract love. Create this powerful little charm on a Friday, the day named for Freya, the Norse Goddess of love, and also sacred to Aphrodite, the Greek Goddess of beauty, independence and love.

YOU'LL NEED:

A red cloth heart

A piece of red velvet or silk large enough to make a small pouch: around 20 cm square will be perfect

A small handful of dried orange peel

A small handful of dried rose petals

A cinnamon quill (or powdered cinnamon is fine)

A few cloves

A small piece of rose quartz or an unpolished ruby or a piece of garnet (each of these has slightly different energy; you choose which works best for you)

Red cotton and a needle

A red ribbon

WHAT TO DO:

❋ After dedicating this working to all that is love, ask for Freya or Aphrodite's blessing for this charm. Take your cloth heart and breathe deeply into it seven times. Whisper words such as the things you wish to have and wish to be. Stay in the energy. Let any sceptical thoughts drift by.

❋ When you have finished charging this heart, place the love energy–charged heart at the centre of the red velvet or silk, then gently cover the heart with your ingredients – the orange for sweetness, joy, health in love, the rose for truth and beauty, the cinnamon for spice and sensuality and the cloves for purification

and healing. Place the crystal or gemstone on last. When you have
completed this, breathe a wish into the pouch. Gather up all the
ends of the fabric and stitch it with the needle and thread into a
little pouch. Sew the pouch together then tie it firmly with the red
ribbon. Tie this three times, saying each time:

> *By the power of three times three*
> *As I do will, so mote it be.*

❋ Hang this magickal pouch over your bed, keep it tucked under your
pillow or wear it under a special outfit. Give it time. Your love is on
their way.

You must remember that when you are working love magick,
free will is of the greatest importance. We do not cast to draw a
specific person. This is a powerful, emotional, volatile area, so it
must be treated with great respect.

❋ CARDS OF LOVE ❋

I recommend using one of my decks for this spell reading, but any oracle or tarot cards you have and love working with will be perfect! We're going to work with the skill of divination for this spell. We're also going to call in a deity. I would suggest working with Aphrodite.

YOU'LL NEED:

A couple of red candles
Luscious red fabric
Rose quartz, unpolished ruby or garnet
Oracle or tarot cards

WHAT TO DO:

* Open your circle, light your candles and arrange your altar. Spread out the red fabric and place the rose quartz on it.

* Shuffle the cards while contemplating your question. When you feel it is the right time, stop and cut the deck. If, for instance, you wish to uncover the blocks within a relationship, split the deck into three piles, turn one pile upside down, put them back together again and reshuffle before dealing out the cards. This method is very effective for revealing where you're stuck, what you may not be aware of or what you may be in denial about.

* When you have put your deck together again, take three cards from the top of the deck and lay them out on the left in a horizontal line then take three cards and lay them out to the right, again in a horizontal line. Take three more cards and lay the first above the lines, the second below the lines and the third to the right of the laid-out cards.

- The set of three cards on the left represents your partner or the person you feel a connection with. The first card you put down indicates their true feelings, the second how they behave towards you in public and the third how their feelings will develop.
- The set on the right represents you. The first card, card four, indicates your true feelings, the second, card five, your public face and how you come across to this person, and the third, card six, the direction in which your own feelings will develop.
- The card above these two groups, card seven, indicates the destiny of this relationship. The card below, card eight, indicates the potential problems, blocks and challenges and the lessons from this union. The card to the right, card nine, will give you guidance regarding right action in this relationship.
- Make notes about your reading in your Grimoire and remember, you've asked for help, real help, and the cards do not lie. Take the advice of Aphrodite.
- Blow out your candles, making a wish on the out breath.
- Close circle.
- Thank Aphrodite for her assistance. Have confidence in her guidance.

❈ Dreaming of Love Pillow ❈

Magickal pillows are fantastic tools. They smell beautiful, hold power and you sleep on them all night, so they're working while you're resting. It also means the magick can get in deep because we are highly open to magick and energy while we sleep.

You'll need:

A handful of rose petals

A handful of dried jasmine

Some sprigs of rosemary

A little sprinkle of lavender flowers

A little sprinkle of chamomile, if you wish

A bay leaf

A few peppercorns

A few drops of essential oils: choose from lavender, rose, rosewood, rose geranium, patchouli

Parchment and a pen with crimson or purple ink

Soft, lovely, deep fabric

Deep red thread and a needle

Note: if you'd like to get really funky, pop in a small piece of dried mango wood. You can find them in Indian stores and they're renowned for their love-drawing magicks.

What to do:

* ❈   Friday is perfect, but if that's not possible any evening will do, especially an evening around 7 pm when the moon is new through to full. I would not recommend doing this spell when the moon is waning.

❀ Gather all the flowers, herbs and the peppercorns and stir them together in a bowl – you can use the mango wood for this. If you have a cauldron to work with, even better.

❀ Take your parchment, write what it is you would love from a relationship and let the words flow. Write your name down frequently and often, too. Sprinkle your essential oil onto your parchment.

❀ While all the ingredients are brewing away, stitch your pillow and with every stitch say a word to do with what you want in a relationship. It could be 'depth', 'fun', 'conversation', 'adventure' or 'passionate kisses'. Remember that with every stitch you are filling your pillow case with love-attracting energy. Leave one short side open so you can fill your pillow.

❀ Pop in all your herbs and spices and stitch up the final side, saying as you do so:

With every stitch
My spell is true
My true love now
I dream of you.

Needles and pins are very magickal objects that really stick the energy into the object, driving it in.

❀ Pop this under your pillow. Your true love will become more and more aware of you. You may even dream of them tonight . . .

Love Goddess Spell

YOU'LL NEED:
A pink, red or orange candle
A heart talisman (you can find lots of these on eBay or in op shops
or use an old piece of jewellery; it's really wonderful if it has some connection to you
personally)
Rose petals
One pink, red or orange charm pouch

WHAT TO DO:
- ❈ On a Friday, go to your altar and cast your magick circle.
- ❈ Using your index finger, cast a circle of light
  around yourself, tracing it in the air.
- ❈ See a beautiful circle of white light protecting, balancing
  and energising you and your magickal space.
- ❈ Call in each of the elements, saying:

I welcome the spirits of the earth, air, fire and water
to this circle. Blessed be!

- ❈ Take your candle and anoint it from top to bottom, then
  carve your name into it along with the word 'love'.
- ❈ Hold the candle to your heart. Feel the love in your heart
  and pour it into your candle, activating your love energy,
  ready to be set alight and sent out into the world.

❋ Say:

By Rhiannon, Ishtar and Aphrodite
I now ignite my love energy
By all the power of three times three
As I do will, so mote it be.

❋ Feel your heart's powerful alluring energy of love and
desirability pouring into your candle. Place it on the altar and
light it, feeling your attractiveness come even more alive.

❋ Take your heart talisman and hold it to your own heart. Say:

By Rhiannon, Ishtar and Aphrodite
A loving heart I draw to me
By all the power of three times three
As I do will, so mote it be.

❋ Place your heart talisman on your altar with the candle. As you
do so, feel the power of your love Goddess spell radiating its
energy out into the world, an ambassador for your heart.

❋ Take the rose petals in your hand and hold them to your heart. Say:

By Rhiannon, Ishtar and Aphrodite
A love so sweet now comes to me
By all the powers of three times three
As I do will so mote it be.

❋ Place your rose petals on your altar beside your heart
talisman and your candle. As you do so, understand that
whoever shall come to you now is for the highest good of all
concerned and that this love will serve your happiness.

✻ Stand with arms outstretched and feel the energy of the planet's unconditional love pouring into you, lighting up your every cell and activating all your potential for true love.

✻ Say out loud in a strong clear voice three times:

I am a beautiful, desirable being.
I am worth loving.
I love. I am loved. I love. I am loved.

✻ When your candle has burned down, take its wax, your heart talisman and your rose petals. Place all three together in your charm bag.

✻ Tie the cord three times. As you do so, say:

Bound around this spell shall be
By all the powers of three times three
My true love now comes to me
As I do will, so mote it be.

✻ Thank and farewell the elements and close your magick circle by pointing your index finger in the direction you began in, tracing your circle in the opposite direction to close and drawing the beautiful energy of the circle back into you.

✻ Ground yourself by eating an apple, the fruit of Aphrodite.

✻ Carry your charm bag on you for the rest of Friday's daylight hours.

✻ On Friday evening, take your heart talisman out of its pouch and wear it around your neck or tuck it into your clothing for at least one week. You may wear it for longer if you wish, but be sure to wear it until the following Friday at the same time you put it on to fully activate its magick.

Beltane Garland

Beltane is the old Celtic and Witches' festival of love and fertility and commitment. This spell can be cast at any time of the year to draw love.

YOU'LL NEED:
Three pieces of a vine-like flowering plant, something really flexible and about a metre long; jasmine is perfect
Some long-stemmed herbs such as rosemary or lavender
Roses, gardenias or any flowers you love
Some little bells, ribbons and fabric

WHAT TO DO:
* Braid the vines, just as you would hair. The braid does not have to be tight – keep it loose and soft but firm enough so they are woven together. As you do so, chant softly:

> *Through this circle love enters anew*
> *Worthy, heartfelt, pure and true*
> *Steadfast, honest, lasting, kind*
> *Into this garland I now bind.*

* Twist or tie the ends of the plait together so you have a beautiful circle. Thread the herbs through the garland and add the flowers. Tie some bells and ribbons onto the vines to get the faeries involved. They are wonderful allies when it comes to love!
* Once you've finished, staying in that strong, loving energy, hang the Beltane garland on your front door. The best times are when there is a new to full moon or on a Friday or, best of all, at Beltane, the traditional day for love and passion in the Witches' calendar: 30 April / 1 May in the northern hemisphere or 31 October / 1 November in the southern hemisphere.

Separation Spell

I developed this spell for a friend who was having a terrible time getting over her ex. My notes in my Grimoire reminded me of how intensely she was suffering. I hope the spell I created for her eases your pain, as it did for her.

It is best to work this spell skyclad (naked), as anything you wear during the casting of it can retain the energy of the relationship. No jewellery, either. Don't bathe until after the spell is completed, after which you will thoroughly cleanse yourself with lemon myrtle soap or a gentle citrus-based cleanser.

YOU'LL NEED:
Some earth and a small clay pot
Clay that is solid enough to shape figures with, enough for at least two small figures
Pen and paper
One small lemon verbena plant
Water, blessed and charged with the intention of cleansing and clearing; it's better if it has been collected during the moon's waning phase or a dark moon (have it handy in a ceremonial chalice or cauldron)

WHAT TO DO:
- ❀ Cast your circle in your usual manner. Within the sacred circle, pour the earth into the pot or onto the ground if you are working in a garden and charge it with healing energy.
- ❀ Still in the centre of your circle, take your clay and forge two figures. These little people now represent you and the person or situation you are moving away from. Pour your emotions into them. Make sure they feel as real as you can make them.
- ❀ Bury your little people deep in the earth.
- ❀ Cover the figures completely with the earth and feel the relationship moving into the past.

* Meditate on moving on and how best you can manifest that goal. When you feel the power peak, take a pen and write down everything you would like to achieve over the following year.
* Once this is completed, ask the Universe to bless your plans.
* Take your little lemon verbena and plant it on top of the figures. Water it with some water from your chalice or cauldron. Know that life is a circle, and that as there is sadness there will be joy; that as there is this winnowing, this cutting away and falling of the dead leaves, so there will be new life and green shoots. Allow the mystery of healing to take place.
* Say three times:

This wheel shall turn.

What you're really affirming is that while this is sad and this is how you feel, that it will change because time and seasons will keep moving and so will you in accord with the natural cycles. You will not stagnate, live on memories or become bitter. You will continue to turn and change too.

* Close your circle by walking widdershins (anti-clockwise in the northern hemisphere, clockwise in the south) around the plant and your buried figures.
* Over time, the clay figures will become one with the earth and nurture the roots of the plant. The pain will be long gone, as will any confusion and regrets or bitterness. From that same earth, new life, new relationships and new adventures will flower and these energies will flow into the healing qualities and powers of the lemon verbena.
* When you can harvest some of your lemon verbena and make some magickal tea for happiness and future dreams (see page 138) you will be healed.

Note: this spell can be adapted to suit any situation such as a job ending, a friendship changing or a household breaking up (say, if your parents are splitting up it could help you to cope with the changes; you just have to modify the figures in the clay-working part of the spell). It can even be used for an actual death, although I truly wish that none of you will have need for it in that regard.

❋ Love Potion Tea ❋

Tea is perhaps the simplest, most effective magickal potion there is. Remember your healing spell where you used lemon verbena? Now you can work with that plant for a relationship bliss tea.

Lemon Verbena Future Bliss Tea

You'll need:

Leaves from your lemon verbena, only a third maximum at any time — the plant will flourish for a bit of clearing! Dry them by laying them out on a dry cloth in a place with good air circulation. Your altar is perfect — maybe just open a window slightly as you don't want the leaves blowing away! Once dry, you can put them in an airtight jar and keep them away from moist environments. Be sure to label them!

What to do:

❋ Use your hands to shred the dry leaves into little pieces. As you do so, say wonderful, soothing words over them such as 'luck', 'good fortune', 'bliss', 'effortless', 'joy', 'ease', 'flow', 'friend' and 'companion'.

❋ Steep a small teaspoonful of leaves in a cup of just-boiled water. Stir them widdershins if you need to remove any bad feelings and stir them deosil if you're ready for some new energy either in your current or new relationship.

❋ Wait till the bliss tea is cool enough to sip, then drink it all up, maybe while writing in your Grimoire.

You can easily blend this herb with others for different effects:

- To bring in romance: two parts lemon verbena, one part rose petals.
- To dream of love: two parts lemon verbena, one part lavender or a touch of mugwort, a herb that induces very insightful and vivid dreams. Only a touch, mind: it is powerful!
- To spice up your love life, to make it more fun: blend lemon verbena and orange zest.
- To purify your love: lemon verbena and lemon zest.
- To bring good cheer: lemon verbena and lime zest.
- To improve your memory: lemon verbena and mint for those of us who forget anniversaries and other romantic dates!

✳ A Ritual Bath to Draw Love ✳

Friday nights are sacred to Aphrodite and Freya, and a great evening to recharge your self-love.

Light a candle and get out your Grimoire. You can write down all your musings about the relationship within its pages. Spend time really noticing your good points and affirm to yourself that you are worth loving and worthy of attracting a wonderful relationship into your life now.

Run yourself a warm bath, light a pink candle and sprinkle seven drops of rose absolute rose otto, rose maroc or rose geranium essential oils into the bathwater.

While bathing by candlelight, think of all the qualities you would like in a partner – it's important and essential to contemplate what you want, not who you want, in this exercise!

Afterwards, put on a beautiful outfit and eat an apple – they're sacred to Aphrodite. Stay really cushioned in that place of love, feeling it soothe, heal and re-energise you.

Once you're in bed, there is room for nothing except blissful, loving thoughts.

This could be a good time, too, to pop a dreaming of love pillow beneath your regular pillows (see page 129).

A Spell to Heal an Argument

YOU'LL NEED:

To mend a friendship with a woman you will need a yam, rounded in shape
To mend a quarrel with a lover use a pear
To mend heartbreak after unfaithfulness use an apple
To mend a friendship with a man use a long yam
A spoonful of honey
Some green thread
Some red thread

WHAT TO DO:

❋ Open your circle.
❋ Call upon the Goddess Hina to mend friendships.
❋ Slice your fruit or yam lengthwise.
❋ Say:

This is our quarrel, our sadness, our parting.

❋ Anoint the centre of each slice with honey and say:

Let misunderstanding end.

❋ Join the two halves together again, letting the honey act as glue, and say:

Let sweetness join us once again.

* Take the green thread and bind the two halves together,
wrapping your choice of fruit or yam nine times.
* Take the red thread and bind the two halves together,
wrapping the fruit or the yam nine times, saying:

Let love between us grow strong once again.

* Place the fruit or yam in the oven set at 180
degrees Celsius until softened.
* Eat the fruit with cream or honey to taste. For the yam, sprinkle it
with salt and enjoy with some soy sauce and garlic for purification
of the relationship. Know that the sweetness of your meal is the
growing return of love and good feelings between you both.
* With the food in your belly, make contact with your friend and let
them know that you are sorry you have quarrelled, and that you wish
to have them returned to your life. Leave the outcome to the God
and the Goddess and know their response is for your highest good.
* Close circle and may your friendship or love,
if it is meant to be, be reborn.

Path-clearing and Forgiveness Spell

YOU'LL NEED:

Your athame or boline

One gold candle and one green candle

Frankincense or incense

Some blessed water

Sea salt

A black pen

Gold paper

A few drops of an essential oil blend of sandalwood and sweet orange

A candle, extra

Frankincense, extra

WHAT TO DO:

❋ Cleanse your home and follow with a smudge stick, then use a ceremonial broom to finish off. Sweep away sadness and any memories you don't want to hold onto anymore. Energy lingers long after people have visited or been around us, so this cleansing is a wonderful way to feel free and utterly ourselves again.

❋ Open the magick circle with your athame to represent the scythe of harvest. It is appropriate to substitute your boline to open circle with at this sabbat, as it reflects the scythe of harvest more closely than even your athame.

❋ Light and lift the candles and say:

I welcome the spirits of fire.

✿ Light and lift the frankincense or incense and say:

I welcome the spirits of air.

✿ Take a sip of the water and say:

I welcome the spirits of water.

✿ Lift the sea salt and say:

I welcome the spirits of the earth.

✿ Run the athame through the smoke of the incense three times so it is thoroughly cleansed and purified by the smoke.
✿ Say aloud:

I now ask for any cords between me and [name of person you wish to be free of here] to be unbound, for us to be free to go our own ways, for us to no longer impact on each other in the way we once did. I am free, and there are no ties that bind us from our past lives, our present lives or in our future lives.

✿ Take the athame, and anywhere you really feel that energetic attachment (it might be in your solar plexus or around your heart region) make a strong but careful cutting motion through the air in front of it, saying:

We are now free. I wish you well but on the past I do not dwell.

- ❄ Reflect on anything you regret about your relationship and write these down with the black pen on gold paper. As you write, sincerely farewell it. If there is anyone or anything you are holding on to, now is the time for letting go of them.
- ❄ Burn your list. Say goodbye with empathy and compassion.
- ❄ Anoint the area that seemed to hold most energy with the oil.
- ❄ Close the circle.
- ❄ Know and truly believe you will move forward. Take strong action to do so. You will find you have more energy and more delight in everyday life once this spell has been worked.
- ❄ Burn a candle anointed with frankincense and encircled widdershins with sea salt to clear any energy in a room or the room where you worked this spell.

Letting Go of Grief Spell

Safely release sadness, anger and emotions with this spell. I would
recommend casting on a Saturday during a waning moon.

YOU'LL NEED:
*Sea salt infused with cloves and frankincense and dragon's blood (if dragon's blood is
hard to find or beyond your budget, bay leaf and black pepper will do)
A few juniper berries
A free-range egg
A black or dark blue candle*

WHAT TO DO:
* Run a beautiful warm bath into which you have scattered three
handfuls of pure rock or sea salt infused with essential oil of
frankincense and with a little ground dragon's blood as well as
the juniper berries. Gently place the whole egg into your tub.
* Light your candle and bathe in its light. Go through any situations
or events or things that were said or done that you're still feeling
resentful about. Feel them and stop judging yourself for having them.
* Let these feelings literally drain out of you and feel them magickally
being pulled into the egg. Feel all lingering feelings stream out of your
feet, through your hands, and flow into the water and into the egg.
When you feel this is final and you are clean and emptied, pull the plug
and you will feel the pain of the past drain from your own body and
mind and emotions and spirit. Then, just to be on the safe side, pop on a
robe, take your egg outside and bury it deep within the earth. Sprinkle
a little salt over it, then fill in the hole with the earth and thank it for
transforming your pain. Now you can move on with your new life.

NOTE:timing is important with this spell. A dear friend did this spell after a devastating break-up and I told her to wait to let the shock subside and to be really clear on what she wanted before casting. She went ahead, though, as she could not wait to be free. She rang me, very shocked, as several days after she'd buried her egg in the garden she found it sitting on top of the earth. Her ex came over and found it, picked it up and threw it over the garden wall! So, things really were over after that and she's never looked back, even though it was extremely challenging at the time. Give yourself a little time after a big break-up before you do the spell.

To Be Desired Blend

This is a powerful, potent and passionate sea salt bath blend.

YOU'LL NEED:

A large and luminous piece of rose quartz

Half a handful of rose petals

A pinch of cloves

Half a handful of rosemary

A cup of sea salt

A cup of pink Himalayan salt

9 drops rose absolute

9 drops sweet orange essential oil

3 drops patchouli essential oil

5 drops white grapefruit essential oil

A silver bowl

A piece of coral or a shell gathered from the shore

A piece of antler, a symbol of Cernunnos

A cinnamon stick

An airtight glass jar

WHAT TO DO:

* ❋ Place all of the ingredients in your silver bowl, and charge with the antler and the coral or shell for some time under a moon that is waxing.
* ❋ Remove your antler piece and coral or shell.
* ❋ Stir deosil, under moonlight, with a cinnamon stick.
* ❋ Keep in an airtight jar until you are ready to use its magick.

Powerful Love Spell – a Return to Love

This is a very effective spell if you have been single for enough time. It is not to be used by those who have recently separated – your energy is different. At least six months must have passed since love has walked out your door, then cast and know love returns. It is to be cast at a full moon to ride that high tide of power and truly liberate and experience within that moment your potential. It is best cast on a Friday or at Beltane, the festival of lusty love, at 7 pm.

You'll need:

A ritual bath blend: make up your preference from the previous spell blends and place in a red charm pouch
4 candles: 2 for the spell, 1 for the fire quarter and 1 for the bath
A small bowl
A bottle of blessed water at eclipse time to break chains and expel doubts and old patterns
Crystals such as rose quartz and unpolished ruby or garnet
Some incense such as frankincense, dragon's blood, rose resin and rosemary (dried and loose)
A charcoal disc and a fireproof container
Salt
A red ribbon anointed with cinnamon and herbs
A piece of large and luminous rose quartz
A red charm pouch
Some chocolate and a pear

What to do:

❋   Prepare first with the ritual bath. This bath is powerful and will cleanse you prior to spellcasting, readying you and clearing any debris of the day.

* Light the first candle during the bath. Inscribe on this candle the rune Gebo, for mutual purpose.

Gebo

* After your bath, consecrate the space you will be using for this spell. Do this in a deosil direction – anti-clockwise in the southern hemisphere, clockwise in the northern. Mark out the four quarters. Below is a suggestion, but please do this in a way that feels right for you.
EAST FOR WATER – place a small bowl with a few drops of the blessed waters of the eclipse.
NORTH FOR FIRE – place one of the candles here.
WEST FOR EARTH – place the crystals here.
SOUTH FOR AIR – light the incense here.
Please do this with charcoal and a fireproof container.

* Purify the area by sprinkling the area with a touch of the blessed eclipse water. Follow this with the salt. Remember to go in a deosil direction.

* Chant three times:

I protect my sacred space
My intent is firm and strong
Guardians keep this holy place
Nothing enters that does not belong.

* Open the circle.
* Awaken each of the elements: pour the water into the bowl, knowing as you do so that you ease your thirst and allow yourself to flow.
* Light the candles and know you ignite your spirit and motivation.
* Light the incense and stir the stir the smoke with your breath, feeling your thoughts grow clear and your breath deep and strong. Feel the space purify.
* Hold the crystals to your heart for a moment and breathe into them, then put them back on the ground/surface. Feel their strength pour

through you and pour yourself into them. Allow the earth to love you and love her in return.

❁   Within this sacred space, say three times as you walk the circle:

Cast a circle round about
Power stay in, world stay out
Cast a circle round about
Magick stay in, world stay out
Cast a circle round about
Guardians stay in, world stay out.

❁   While standing in this space, take a deep breath in. Feel the presence of the Goddess.

❁   Take two candles and inscribe your name upon them, and upon the other simply write 'beloved'.

❁   Inscribe underneath your name the rune for Wunjo, or joy. Underneath the 'beloved' inscribe the rune for Jera for fertility and harvest. Say with great sincerity:

Wunjo   Jera

I wind this ribbon this heart around
I soften ties that once were bound
I no longer look, for all is found
Beloved and truth, freedom and health
Courage bright, spirit and wealth.

❁   Wind the ribbon around the rose quartz, leaving a little to loop around the candles.

❁   Say with conviction and passion and humility:

Aphrodite, come to me
I cast this spell in praise of thee
I honour you with breath and vow
I call to you to help me now
Bring me courage, sweet and true
In return I promise you
I will honour my flesh and bone
Whether Maiden, Mother, Crone
I will love myself divine
Until a lover's arms entwine
He will be strongand loyal and true
He will recall the Goddess who
Wove us together, heart to heart
A lifetime together, never to part
Before this truth can come to be
I must now devote myself to me
And in this time of loving self
I will win my soul's true health
Passion, joy and courage bright
I ignite with you this night
Now you hear my sacred vow
As I wish it, be it now
As I wish it, be it now
As I wish it, be it now.

❁ Write down a list of commitments to Aphrodite such as no more judgement of your sensuality, praise and love of self, dignity and honour in love, freedom in choice of partner.

❁ Wait a moment to hear any messages from the Goddess Aphrodite. Write them down.

❁ Let the candles burn down and know the spell is working.

❀ Say any wishes or dreams you have regarding love out loud.

❀ Make statements of intent and thank the Goddess, then say:

By moonlight I cast this spell
Into me now your power swells
I thank you now and welcome all
This new life brings, I hear your call.

❀ Place the crystals in the red charm pouch and thank the earth, then place within it the waters (just a sprinkle will do) and thank the water. Place within it a little of the incense and thank the air, then place within it a little wax and thank the fire. Finally place within it the rose quartz and the ribbon.

❀ As you tie the pouch off say:

The power of this spell within me
As I do will, so mote it be
As I do will, so mote it be
As I do will, so mote it be.

❀ It is time to thank and farewell this circle. Trace the circle round in the opposite direction to that which you cast it in, saying:

My circle is open, but never is it broken. My circle is open,
but never is it broken.

❀ Take a moment to breathe and feel the energy shifting.

❀ Clear the area of all tools and items and vacuum up the salt or sweep it up and clear it all.

❀ Eat some chocolate or a pear for grounding.

❀ Carry your pouch for a moon cycle or for longer. Pop it under your pillow. After one lunar cycle, take the ribbon and tie it to a fast-growing branch of a healthy, flowering tree.

CHAPTER 12

Protection Spells

We all have people and special keepsakes that we want to protect. We also need to protect ourselves from time to time. You'll find here several tried and well-tested spells – they'll break curses and shield you from negativity, repel attacks and keep you from harm. Treat these spells like your rainy day clothes or a crash helmet. They go a long way towards ensuring you'll get through a risky time safe and sound, body and soul.

Spells also work on a psychological level. What this means is that they give us the means and confidence to take steps to protect ourselves. Thus our energy shifts and we are no longer attracting the same kind of negative behaviour.

Dark Moon Spell

You will need to cast this spell during a dark moon in order for it to be most effective. You are not ill wishing; you are dissolving, transmuting and casting off ties to those qualities.

YOU'LL NEED:
A black candlez
A piece of charcoal
Some juniper berries
A handful of salt
A handful of lemon verbena

WHAT TO DO:
❃ Open your circle.
❃ On the black candle, write the names of the traits and qualities in yourself you no longer wish to see in your life. It is best to focus on qualities you wish to change in yourself. The clearer you are the more powerful this will be.
❃ Set up the black candle in a candleholder so it is secure and light it.
❃ Light the charcoal piece and burn the juniper berries on it.
❃ Let the candle burn down completely. If you must leave the room, close the door behind you firmly. It is important to contain this energy.
❃ Store the melted wax with the salt and bury it in the garden or a pot of earth. Sprinkle the lemon verbena over the top.
❃ Close your circle.

Removal of Psychic Attack

This spell is to be cast at a waning moon or a dark moon for the removal of psychic attack.

YOU'LL NEED:

A teaspoon of dried juniper berries
A bay leaf
A piece of dragon's blood
A ground cinnamon stick
Rosemary, dried or fresh
Some charcoal discs
A cauldron or fireproof container
Athame (optional)

WHAT TO DO:

* Go to your sacred space. Don't wash, and don't try to feel good. Be real. Be authentic.
* Cast your circle.
* Sit down. Please, don't ask for protection at this stage. You want everything to be very clean, open and clear.
* Bring into your mind and say out loud the qualities of those people who have hurt you either through intent or ignorance or lack of understanding.
* Combine your herbs and stir them widdershins. This is your banishing blend.
* Light the charcoal discs and place on a protective surface or in your cauldron.
* Place the herbs on them and let them smoke. Scoop the smoke into your hands and move it about your body, moving your entire self

through the smoke. Once this is done, stand and imagine anyone or anything you feel may have harmed you standing with you, cords extending from you to them. Blow the smoke towards them and see the cords fade and dissolve as the smoke clears them.

* Now ask for the Goddess Brigid to come in and slice the cords and do some energetic surgery to heal swiftly any wounds made during the releasing process. You may wish to use your athame during this process, cutting through energetic cords as you are guided.

* Once you are finished, put out the burning herbs. Sit still and breathe until you feel calm and centred and clear.

* Close your circle.

Super-sensitive Empath Protection Spell

If you are an empathetic person you're probably compassionate, intuitive, helpful and very understanding. You also probably need some protection. This spell will assist with stress from other people's emotions and feeling like the world, schoolwork, family, relationships and friends are just too much to deal with. Don't withdraw – let's protect you and get you healthy again, energetically!

YOU'LL NEED:
A beeswax candle
A small handful of sea salt
3 generous drops of sandalwood oil
A maidenhair fern

WHAT TO DO:
❋ Find yourself a calm, quiet and secluded place
where you can be alone for 20 minutes.
❋ Light the beeswax candle and surround it with the sea salt, trickling
it clockwise if you are in the southern hemisphere and anti-clockwise
if you are in the northern. Run a soothing warm bath and add the
sandalwood oil. Bless the waters with clearing salt. Hold a handful of sea
salt and say:

May the waters wash away my fears and allow me to feel emotionally clear,
clean and flowing.

❋   Hold the sea salt and say:

May the power and purity of fire burn away my fears and terror and bring me passion and motivation.

Turn and say:

May the power of earth transform any illness or disease within my physical self, replacing these with stability, sound support and growing well-being.

❋   Finally, turn and say:

May the air clear my thoughts and grant me a peaceful mind and inspiring thoughts.

❋   After you have done this, step into the bath and cleanse yourself. After you have bathed, dry yourself with a big soft towel.
❋   Plant the maidenhair fern in a sheltered place and water it regularly. As it flourishes, so shall you. Neglect it, and know that you must tend your own needs again. Its health will be a barometer of your own. You will grow so strong yet you will remain sensitive. It can be done!
❋   Remember, these directions are for the southern hemisphere east coast. Change them so they work with where you live.

Stop Spell

One of my first and most simple spells came from a very old book on magick.
It told of an ancient way to peacefully stop another being from hurting you.
Write their name on a piece of parchment and place it under the snow.
The result? That particular person would be prevented from harming anyone.
I live in very hot, very sunny Australia and I wondered if a freezer would
work just as well.

One day, after being pushed to my limit, I cleared my mind of my emotions,
and with love in my heart I wrote a name on a piece of paper. I focused on
keeping my mind clear and wishing this person only good as I placed the
piece of paper into a glass of water and then into the freezer, and said:

By all the powers of three times three
I wish only good to come to thee
I wish thee well, strong and happy
And very far away from me.

It worked: slowly, safely and in a very subtle way. We were not parted
but it was as if we never truly connected again — and the bullying I was
experiencing ceased.

Inanna Spell for Justice, Protection and Strength

This spell will help you find justice and calls on the ancient Goddess of Sumeria, Inanna. If you feel angry, hurt and betrayed this will help you claim justice, lessening any shame you may feel. Confusion can also dissipate as a result of calling on Inanna.

Do not act impulsively on urges to wound, retaliate and hurt, but channel the force behind the emotion into constructive change and the motivation to stand up and refuse to back down.

WHAT TO DO:

* Open your circle.
* Recite part of the ancient hymn to Innana, written down in 2300 BCE by a priestess of Innana, Enheduanna of Ur or ancient Sumeria. It's the oldest known piece of prose by a woman. It is a powerful and very honest cry to a great Mother Goddess of an ancient, splendid culture. Feel her power and take action with your own.

O, queen of the seven Gods, o, radiant splendour
Of light, fountain of life, darling of heaven
My honey sweet voice is hoarse and strident
And all that gave me pleasure has fallen to dust.
I, what am I among living creatures!
An, An, give to punishment the rebels
Who hate Inanna, and split their cities' walls!
Priestess, queen, noble commander of Gods,
Destroyer of barbarians, whom An made protector of spirits,
Queen, clothed in allure and attraction, Inanna: praise!

* Connect with the force of your anger and see yourself channel it into action that has healthy outcomes. Innana will be with you for a time – and you may also wish to call upon Kali and Brigid to offer you their protection. You are not alone. Draw an eight-pointed star in the air over yourself or draw it on your body, on each shoulder, to invoke Inanna's assistance and positive intervention.
* Close your circle.

Banish Bad Dreams Spell

There is no need to cast circle for this working.
Many of us have nightmares and they can hit very hard when we are
between nine and around 27 years old. It's a tough time for many, but there
are protective measures you can take that will diminish their frequency.
Some nightmares are practice runs for things we need to face in our daily
lives, while other nightmares can be the result of negative energy being sent
our way, manifesting in the dream state when we are more vulnerable.

YOU'LL NEED:
4 small pieces of obsidian
A small handful of sea salt
An onion (red, white or brown)

WHAT TO DO:
❋   Place a small piece of obsidian and some salt around each leg of your
bed. Do this in the widdershins direction – anti-sunwise in your part
of the world. The sun moves clockwise in the north and anti-clockwise
in the southern hemisphere. Most important of all is that you place the
salt there. Also sprinkle a little along the windowsills in your bedroom.
❋   Slice the onion in half and place one half on the windowsill
of your room and another by your front door. Onions absorb
impurities, are blood cleansers and are really powerful magickally,
so when you place this onion and this salt on your windowsill
nothing is going to get past. Leave the onion and salt there for
three days and nights, then thoroughly clean the area.

✼ Replace the salt under your bed regularly and you will find the dreams and night terrors will diminish. Provide yourself with a nurturing environment by putting on some soothing meditation music to listen to before you sleep.

✼ Please do not buy a cheap dreamcatcher from a shop. If you wish to work with a dreamcatcher for a powerful spellcasting, make your own or purchase one from someone who is a brilliant energy worker and who makes them brimming with energy. The ones you get from the very cheap shops often have been manufactured in factories or sweatshops and their energy is not good!

Banishing Pentagram Protection

This is to protect your home from robbery while you're away. I have used this spell for more than 20 years, without fail, when I leave my home for more than a day or so. I travel a lot and I live in a high-crime inner-city area, so I do it consciously every time. It works.

Before you leave your home, raise your sending hand – if you're right-handed it's that hand – and draw a pentagram in the air over the window, like you're blasting electricity out through your fingertips and it's gathering over the entry to your home. Start your pentagram at your lower left then up to the right if you're in the southern hemisphere. Go the opposite way in the northern. Why? Because that's how you draw a banishing pentagram. Do it three times, really smoothly. Draw a circle, widdershins, around the banishing pentagram and see it begin to spin in your mind's eye. I do this on the doors and windows to my home and it works just like an energetic lock.

If you just want to protect something private or an object such as your phone or your book of shadows and light, you draw the banishing pentagram over it. It will protect it from anyone else. I really suggest you get into a habit with doing this – sure it looks a little odd to the taxi driver out front as I do it on the door once I've closed it, but it is so worthwhile.

If you wish to add a little extra protection, draw in your mind's eye a circle of blue fire around your home, room, heart – whatever it is you wish to protect. All that is safe and that wishes you well will move through the blue fire unharmed and perfectly unaware of the energy there. Anyone with any malintent will not make a move towards you or towards anything that is precious to you.

Dark Moon Bath Blend

Blend and bless this at the sunset of a dark moon. This blend will release, remove and dissolve ties that you may have to difficult people and give you the strength to let go of those you find yourself unable to let go of. It is powerful and it will clear energies.

You'll need:
Sea salt or glacier salt
Frankincense resin or oil
A small handful of juniper berries
A bay leaf
An oak leaf
A small handful of sage
Sandalwood and orange
A piece of black tourmaline
A silver or dark-coloured bowl
A banishing pentagram – this can be drawn over the blend or you can use an actual pentacle and lay it on the blend for about three minutes, drawing it in your mind's eye in the banishing direction and energised with a silver banishing pentagram
A rowan or eucalypt stick

What to do:
* Place all in a bowl. Meditate on the banishing pentagram, then stir, widdershins, at least nine times with a rowan or eucalypt stick. Stir in multiples of three.
* Place a pinch in your wash to clear any energies remaining from your clothes.
* Throw a few handfuls of the blend into the bath, soak, release and be free! Work with this any time the emotional attachment and the desire arises to reconnect to those who are not good for you or

substances or situations that are not good for you. This will help you really overcome temptation and be very healthy in your emotional, spiritual and physical choices – and, of course, thinking more clearly and freely is also supported when you work with this blend.

Releasement Blend II

B lend as the sky darkens from blue to black. Just after sunset and just before full dark is a good time to do this. This is another variation of a very dependable blend that cuts through remnant energetic ties to difficult people and releases old patterns. It can also lift energy blocks and even remove entities. Place a pinch or two in the wash to protect you even further.

You'll need:
Sea salt or glacier salt
A mortar and pestle
Resin of frankincense
A small quantity of dragon's blood resin
A small handful of dried sage
A dried bay leaf
A single juniper berry
Essential oil of frankincense
Smoky quartz

What to do:
  * Run a deep, warm bath.
  * Cast three handfuls of the blend into your bath.
  * Bathe and know that any energetic remnants are being cleansed and cleared. After this bath you will feel freer, lighter and stronger.

Stop Gossip Spells

These types of spells almost deserve their own category – speaking ill of others has always been an issue wherever you have people gathered together. That is why the Greeks have their evil eye charm and why most cultures have a way of removing this influence. The reason it has been so important to humans is that gossip and cruel rumours do hurt people, change lives and can destroy confidence. There are many philosophical ways of dealing with this issue: for example, there is the saying, 'What others think about me is none of my business.' I agree, but what others do to you and when they target you with harmful action, it is your business.

Here's how to use some magickal jujitsu to shift the energy and have those enemies toppling, leaving you – and most likely vulnerable others – be. You will need to be calm, clear and still when casting these spells. You will need to be centred and have courage too. If you find yourself shaking with rage and hurt, make sure you wait until the peak of intensity of emotion has passed before you cast. You can feel – that's fine – it's energy, but if your feelings are ruling you you won't cast effectively. It is always best to be in this powerful, centred place when you cast. In this spell you are going to make use of some of the very oldest Witches' tools – bottles, binding thread and poppets (small dolls that represent real people).

Bottle and Binding Spell

YOU'LL NEED:
A pinch of clay
A length of black thread
Some salt
A pinch of black pepper
Some juniper berries
Some parchment
A pin
A pen
A small bottle with a stopper

WHAT TO DO:

❋ Cast your circle.

❋ On a waning or dark moon, write down the name of the person who has said untrue and unfair things of you. Make a model of their mouth with the clay. Take the black thread and tie up the mouth. Really close it tight. This will not harm the person; it will, however, make them feel very uncomfortable whenever they go to say something untrue or unkind about you, to you or behind your back. They will feel as if their words get stuck.

❋ As you bind the mouth say three times:

Speak no evil, speak no ill, about me now your lips are still.

For a stronger effect you chant this nine times.

❀ Remember the law of three times three. You are not hating them, even if you truly feel that way at times. The place to have those feelings is not within the spellcasting. What you are doing is disciplining them and altering their behaviour.

❀ Sprinkle the lips with the salt, black pepper and juniper berries, then take your parchment and push the pin gently through it and into the mouth. The pin will help bind the spell, making sure the problem will not happen again.

❀ If you do not know the person, simply write down actions and behaviours on the parchment. Place it in the bottle, put in the stopper and bury it in the earth. Some folks like to bury it far away. Personally, I bury it near me as I am taking responsibility for dealing with it. When you do any part of this spell, have no hatred towards the person. Have a very clean, clear, action-oriented energy – like a martial artist or warrior.

❀ If, and this is a very big if, you wish for the energy to change between you and these people, place some honey on the outside of the bottle. Plant a sweet flowering plant with thorns, like a rose, in the earth over the bottle to transform the energy, but now it has a strong boundary. In time they may say wonderful things about you, but my hope is that you will become indifferent to what they say and that you find good friends elsewhere. Of course, friendships do go through their stages but a true friend, even if you part on poor terms, will not spread vicious rumours. They may confide in ones close to them about you and they may criticise you. This is not what we are talking about. Know the difference.

Be Silent Spell Bottle

Here's another bottle spell to catch unpleasant energy.

YOU'LL NEED:
A small bottle with a stopper
Some small pieces of hematite, obsidian, onyx or smoky quartz

WHAT TO DO:
✳ Cast your circle and focus and still your emotions, become very clear and calm, open your bottle and say three times or nine times:

Be silent
Be still
I wish you no ill
Into this your words of hate
Fall harmless and dissipate
They are gone, they do no harm
I move on, this is my charm.

✳ Place a few pieces of hematite, obsidian, onyx or smoky quartz
(all are very good and very protective, with slightly different energies
but similar qualities for the purpose of this spell) into the bottle.
✳ Keep the bottle open and place it near your door or an entranceway so
it can catch anything nasty being sent your way. After three days, when
the energy has been captured, stopper up the bottle. If the energy starts
again, open the bottle up, pop some salt in it and repeat the process.

Sekhmet Banishing Beads

Banishing beads are used in many ancient spells. The lioness-headed Egyptian Goddess Sekhmet has and can connect you with great strength, vitality and ferocity. She is protective, maternal and fierce and will shield you from harm.

If you desire to banish someone from your life it may be best to remove their influence and focus on the behaviour rather than the person. Of course, there are always exceptions – if you feel in any danger from an obsessive ex or someone who feels dangerous, take protective steps within the law, alerting teachers and authorities to any danger you may feel.

I recommend beads of obsidian, garnet, hematite, bloodstone and unpolished ruby. Think of reds and blacks. A small statue or image of Sekhmet nearby as you work on your altar will provide protection and strength. You need three lots of the five different beads, with an extra one to separate each group of five. To complete this set of banishing beads you will need 18 beads in total. Find scarab and statuary type beads online or in museum shops.

You'll need:
A statue or image of Sekhmet
18 beads made of semi-precious crystals, including a scarab bead, a lioness bead and a cobra bead
A length of beading wire

What to do:
* ❂ Cast your circle.
* ❂ With the Sekhmet image before you, call to her with a roar from within and begin threading beads on beading wire. After the first five thread on your scarab bead, then continue. After the next five thread on the lioness, then after the final five thread on the cobra bead.
* ❂ Close your circle.
* ❂ When you feel worried, take the beads and ask Sekhmet for protection. Hang them by your bed and carry them in the day.

It's not always at school or at work that we are bullied. Sometimes it's the people closest to us that we need protection from. If it is a brother or sister or a parent you need protection from the same steps apply, but if there is something that needs to be done and if your parent or sibling is stepping outside what is good and right, seek help from a counsellor or legal officer. This can be very confronting. Here is an oil blend to help us to be brave when we simply must be our own hero.

Courage Oil Blend

An oil blend with a base of almond, jojoba or hazelnut oil with essential oils of fennel, spruce, rosewood, frankincense, sweet orange and blue tansy. Other blend suggestions include enhancing your base oil with rosewood as this will ground and calm you, which is very important when feeling aroused and confronted and fearful.

You can try oak moss — it is one of my favourite essential oils. I love its aroma, but what I enjoy is how it gives you the capacity to imagine different ways of solving problems and tackling issues. It gives you emotional intelligence, which is something, when coupled with courage, that can bring wonderful results.

You can also use this as a magickal wash for clothes by adding a few drops of this oil to your wash. Your clothes will emanate a strength and confidence that you will feel become more and more a part of you and this, in turn, will change the reaction of all those about you.

Self-acceptance Spell

If you have been hurt it is extremely important to take back your power and focus on the wonderful qualities you do have. Those who are most sensitive are often intelligent and creative and have so much to offer the world. We do not want to lose you, so stay strong, work your magick, do what must be done and be yourself. This is temporary. It will change.

WHAT TO DO:
❋ Open your circle.
❋ Hold a mirror up to your face and whisper words of love and apology for allowing yourself to think badly of yourself. Promise this is to be no more. Respect and self-love are paramount and the first steps towards a life well lived.
❋ Close your circle.
❋ Repeat until you lose your self-consciousness and you begin to know your worth and feel healed.

To Break a Bad Habit

Whatever your bad habit is it has created a chemical pathway in your brain that makes it difficult to shift or change or stop. To combat this we can use essential oils, which cut a new chemical pathway into your brain and work very quickly. These oils can also alleviate stress and promote confidence and relaxation and determination that isn't frantic or exhausted easily.

To start, use the number five as it promotes change. Combine five drops of sandalwood oil (it breaks negativity), five drops of lavender (for calm relaxation and extra oxygenation to the brain) and five drops of neroli (which will help you associate change with positive and cheerful consequences).

Add one part of the oil blend to three parts of a carrier oil (like almond or peach) for a body oil. To use in an oil burner, drop a few drops of oil in the top. Burn it when you know you'll be tempted to do whatever it is you do not want to do! As long as what you are giving up is in your best interests, this oil blend will work wonderfully.

To Move a Disturbing Spirit or Entity Along

There are times when we can feel something in our environment like a spirit or entity who just won't leave. Of course, you can cleanse and banish, but you can also make use of this traditional spell and make a spirit bottle and offer the being a new home so you and the spirit can peacefully co-exist.

YOU'LL NEED:
Some feathers, twigs, dried flowers, wood, a crystal such as obsidian and some cotton wool
A large bottle

WHAT TO DO:
* Gently place your ingredients in a sizeable pretty bottle.
* Ask the spirit to come forward, and when you feel their presence show them the new home you have created for them.
* Place the bottle in the garden or suspend it from a tree. Make sure it is secure! We do not want to harm this spirit.
* The lovelier you make it the more likely it is that the spirit will move from your space and into its new home. The comfier it is the less you'll see it. Don't stopper the bottle.

Hair Spell for Protection

If you have long hair, gather a lock of it and plait it. With every plait or Celtic knot you make you are binding good fortune, love, delight, wisdom and protection – all the good things you wish for – into your hair. This always works really well for anyone you wish to protect. Just plait their hair to a count of nine, whispering under your breath all the good things you wish for them – and for you, too, as the spell will affect you also. I did this for my child for years as they headed off to school!

Here's the original spell, called the Witches' ladder spell – you may wish to take these words and rework them slightly for your intent.

By knot of one the spell's begun
By knot of two the spell is true
By knot of three we blessed be
By knot of four the open door
By knot of five the spell's alive
By knot of six this spell I fix
By knot of seven the power is given
By knot of eight and hand of fate
By knot of nine this spell shall shine!

Seal off the plait with a hair band bound three times, repeating:

As I do will so mote it be!

Simple, pretty and very very effective. You're protected and the energy and focus is strong!

Protection Stones and Shells

A long time ago hag stones were not only considered to be the most wonderful way of seeing the otherworld (you peered through the hole and into the world beyond the veil), but they also were considered to have strong protective powers.

YOU'LL NEED:

A stone with a natural hole in the middle of it (keep a look out and you'll find one when the time is right)
Shells with natural holes in them
A piece of fishing line

WHAT TO DO:

* Thread the stones and shells onto your fishing line. You can make it as pretty and appealing as you wish.
* Hang it outside the front door or the back door. The harmful energies will slip through the holes and into the world between the worlds, where they will be cared for.

CHAPTER 13

Spells for Success, Power and Abundance

Money is a very loaded subject in our culture. We want it but we feel guilty about having it. We obtain it and we waste it. We think without it we are powerless. And we allow imaginary money – credit – to send us into debt. Money is a form of energy, and it represents what we have put our energy into – and money is energy we then pour into something. Over time I have developed some very effective money spells to help us all have more power, success, independence and self-determination.

Simple Success Spell

This spell will leave you awash with success.

You'll need:

A beeswax candle
Two tablespoons of honey
A few pieces of citrine
A small handful of dried mint
A few marigold flowers
A small handful of elderflowers and leaves

What to do:

* ❅ Carve an image of a little bee into your candle. Anoint your candle with a little of the honey, then drive the citrine pieces into the base around the outside of the candle. While you are decorating your candle, run a warm bath.

- Light your candle and set it up near your bathtub.
- Sprinkle your prosperity herbs over the bathwater.
- Gaze at the waters, see the magick of the herbs moving into the water and say:

Bee of honey
Bee of health
Bring to me deserved wealth
Bee of wisdom
Druid's bee
Bring prosperity unto me.

- Say your name three times.
- Get into the bath. Think of all the good things you'll do with the prosperity coming your way. Rub the honey into your feet, your hands and your forehead and know that your every footstep creates wealth and sweetness, as does the work of your hands and the products of your thoughts. Wash the honey from you, but know that traces of its golden, sweet and sticky energy will cling to you, drawing success and money.
- Dry off, feeling abundant and brimming with good fortune.

Plant a Money Tree

When I've travelled I've seen so many variations on the money tree. They're often found covered in coins, with symbols of blessings and longevity such as deer and turtles living in the branches – it's kind of a tree heaven where your every need is provided for! My money tree has always brought good fortune and prosperity.

You'll need:

Somewhere to plant your money tree: make sure it's positioned somewhere you will go every day and give it plenty of room to grow as you prosper, as the way you treat your money tree will influence your finances

A healthy tree or a succulent plant for good fortune

Water blessed at a waxing or full moon so it has the energy of expansion and increase

10 gold coins

6 pieces of citrine

Symbols of prosperity and good fortune such as little coins tied to the ends of the branches or toy animals that you love; be inspired in your imaginings

What to do:

* Cast your circle.
* Dig a hole for your tree, feeling yourself clearing away and transforming all that separated you from your abundance.
* Sprinkle some blessed water into the hole.
* Touch the roots of the plant with the coins and the citrine, then put five of each into the hole for the plant. Before planting say three times:

> *From little things big things grow*
> *Into this earth the coins are sewn*
> *From rich soil and blessed water*
> *I stand here now, Fortuna's daughter.*

(If you are a man say:)
From this rich soil abundance comes
I stand here now, Fortuna's son.

* Plant your magickal money tree and fill in the hole with rich earth.
* Place five coins around the plant and another piece of citrine to inspire prosperity. Multiples of five stimulate change and a change in fortune is on its way.
* Close your circle.
* Be sure to nurture your plant with the certainty that you are abundant. Always share the wealth in the form of helping others and share the plant, as she will have many shoots and take root in many places!

Fortune and Fae Spell

Traditionally humans have gone to the faerie kingdom for help with health, healing and good fortune, as well as matters of love. I have found them to be very generous helpers.

On a waxing moon, head out at night. In a little cup, eggshell, leaf or nutshell place some bread and honey and sprinkle with milk or cream. Hold it up for the faeries to see and sense. Call to them and offer them your service in cleaning up and caring for the environment. Ask them for assistance, and leave the offering out for the faeries!

Do this regularly and you will find money comes to you in lucky and very unexpected ways. Just be sure to keep your word and clean up, recycle more and do regular litter pick-ups to keep the balance.

Money-drawing Oil Blend

This blend is a little messy and sticky but it's effective and works quickly – money will literally stick to you.

You'll need:

A few drops of bergamot oil

A teaspoon of manuka honey

A pinch of cinnamon, powdered

A cinnamon stick

A dark glass jar to store the money drawing blend (green is best)

What to do:

❋ Stir this blend up deosil with a cinnamon stick and store in a glass jar. Rub a little on your wallet, money box, calendar and diary. Dab a little on your wrists before applying for a job or any time you have money matters to discuss.

Money-management Spell

What you do with money when it comes to you is going to determine your future prosperity. To reinforce your intent, take magickal action. When the moon is new, tie three green ribbons around a branch of a flowering tree. At its roots, bury three coins. When the tree flowers or shoots above that point where you have tied the ribbons you will have made good use of your money and saved a little nest egg.

Harvest Spell

This spell is one of the oldest in my Grimoires and is simple and perfect for Lughnasadh, or any time you need to give thanks for blessings.

You'll need:
A stick of vanilla incense
A silver coin
A piece of orange fabric
Two green candles anointed with neroli oil
Flowers and sprigs of fast-growing herbs

What to do:

* Sitting at your altar, light the incense. Take the silver coin and wrap it in the piece of orange fabric. Place this on your altar.

* Put the green candles anointed with neroli essential oil on either side of the coin wrapped in orange fabric. Light the candles. Concentrate on the silver coin and visualise your dream coming true in the present, not at a future time. Say three times:

> *As the waves of the ocean are infinite*
> *As the trees in the forest grow tall*
> *Let my work now bring me to harvest*
> *I'm ready to receive my all.*

* Shift your focus to the orange cloth and understand that harvest is coming. Blow out the candles, first right, then left, and place flowers and sprigs of fast-growing herbs around your magickal space.

New Moon, New Beginnings Spell

This is the perfect spell to give you a little extra juice to help you go forward in your life. If you think you can do better with abundance and your ability to generate money as an energy you have a lot to gain from casting this beautiful spell.

You'll need:

A blend of bergamot, oak moss and sandalwood oils – a few drops each

2 candles

A small silver bowl

Blessed water made during a waxing or full moon

Crystals for earth (citrine is best)

Incense

A charcoal disc and a fireproof container

A small handful of salt

A charm pouch

What to do:

❋   Prepare first with a prosperity ritual bath. You need some bergamot, a little oak moss and sandalwood oils.

❋   Light a candle during the bath. Inscribe on this candle the ogham Duir, for oak. Add beneath it the rune Dagaz, for increase and expansion (see the illustration).

❋   After your bath, take yourself to the space you intend to cast. Make sure you have peace, quiet and privacy for about 10 minutes.

❋   Cast your circle.

❋   To honour water: place a bowl with a few drops of the blessed waters of a waxing or full moon, or an eclipse if you've really been stuck for a while!

* To honour fire: place the inscribed candle somewhere safe in your sacred space. Do not light yet.
* To honour earth: place the crystals in your sacred space.
* To honour air: place the incense, charcoal and a fireproof container in your sacred space.
* Cast your circle by sprinkling the area with a touch of the blessed water in a circle. Follow this with the salt. Remember to go in a deosil direction.
* Chant three or nine times:

I protect my sacred space
My intent is firm and strong
Guardians keep this holy place
Nothing enters that does not belong.

* Awaken in turn each of the elements: pour the water into the bowl, knowing as you do so that you ease your thirst. Allow yourself to flow. Say a few words about water and what it means to you. Simply speak from the heart, naturally, letting it flow or fall or falter as it will. There are no mistakes.
* Light the candles and know you ignite your spirit and motivation. Speak of fire and passion.
* Hold the crystals to your heart for a moment and breathe into them, then put them back on the ground or a flat surface. Feel their strength pour through you and pour yourself into them. Allow the earth to love you, and love her in return. Speak to the earth. Share from the heart. Ask the earth to be with you.
* Light the incense and stir the smoke with your breath, feeling your thoughts grow clear and your breath deep and strong. Feel the space purify.
* Say a few words about air and what it means to you. Speak to the air of your feelings and insights. Ask the air to be with you.

❊   Within this sacred space chant these words as you walk, doing this three times or nine times:

> *Cast a circle round about*
> *Power stay in, world stay out*
> *Cast a circle round about*
> *Magick stay in, world stay out*
> *Cast a circle round about*
> *Guardians stay in, world stay out.*

❊   While standing in this space, take a deep breath in. Feel the presence of the sacred. Notice who seems to be with you. How does the energy feel? Say:

> *By new moonlight I cast this spell*
> *Into me now your power swells*
> *I thank you now and welcome all*
> *This new life brings, I hear your call.*

❊   Go to the water section and place some of the water to your forehead and to your feet. Say:

> *I allow my good to flow*
> *When opportunity comes I will know*
> *I cast the shadows far behind*
> *And to me now abundance binds.*

❊   Go to the fire section and carve the symbols for Onn, Ailm and Luis into the candle and light it.

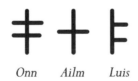

Onn   Ailm   Luis

❉ Say:

> Sacred trees, burning bright
> Protect me now, day and night
> Give me work that's good and strong
> Where I prosper, thrive and do belong.

❉ Go to the crystals and make a grid, following your intuition. Say:

> These crystals here now speak to me
> Of abundance and sovereignty
> I can dream into reality
> Prosperity, community
> My choices grow, the money comes
> To support and create this life I've won.

❉ Go to the incense and blow the smoke, scooping it up and over you. Say:

> My mind is full of ideas anew
> Bright and strong and they acrrue
> I always have so much to share
> And when I do they listen and care!

❉ Come back to the centre and say:

> I now declare myself to the Goddess as I am. I wish you to help
> make me what I am meant to become. To shape me into the things
> that will best serve you and the world. To yield and grow fruit
> and prosper and shine. To bring myself and my loved ones food
> and sustenance and abundance and nurture.

❋ State what you would like the Mother to hear and help you with – specifically. Debts? Giving up bad spending habits? Drawing a better wage? A new job? A flow of abundance to cover all your needs and more? Ask! Name it. Tell her!

❋ Breathe in, and release.

❋ Full of restated and reclaimed purpose, pick up the crystals, put them in the charm pouch and thank the earth. Place within it a sprinkle of the waters and thank the water. Place within it a little of the incense and thank the air. Place within it a little wax and thank the fire.

❋ Imagine a sacred tree growing coins, showering you with the fruits of abundance through your sincere and purposeful efforts and creativity. As you tie the pouch off say:

> *The power of this spell within me*
> *By sacred Goddess and sacred tree*
> *By ocean far and fire bright*
> *By air that sings and earthly delight*
> *Prosperity and plenty now are mine*
> *They come direct from source divine*
> *I bind this spell by three times three*
> *As I do will, so mote it be*
> *As I do will, so mote it be*
> *As I do will, so mote it be.*

❋ It is time to thank and farewell this circle for now. Trace the circle round in the opposite direction to that which you cast it in, saying:

Unwind, unwind as it is spoken
My circle is open
Yet never broken.

⁜ Take a moment to breathe and feel the energy shifting and all that golden energy coming towards you. You're a money magnet!

⁜ Clear the area of all tools and items, vacuum or sweep up the salt and clear it all away.

⁜ Eat something very nourishing and grounding and clean and alive that is the colour gold. So, a mango, pawpaw, orange or sweet potato – although they all have different energy, the most important aspect here is the colour gold!

⁜ Carry your pouch on you for a moon cycle or for longer. Pop some gold coins in it from time to time and have lots of Earl Grey or Lady Grey tea. Bergamot attracts prosperity and really helps keep your mind stay fresh and clever, which will enable you to take advantage of any opportunities to create abundance.

⁜ Pop the pouch under your pillow.

⁜ After one lunar cycle the magick will have firmly taken root and will be beginning to manifest in the world.

High Tide of Psychic Power

This ritual bath salt blend will help really expand your power.

You'll need:

Some frankincense resin

Some jasmine resin

A mortar and pestle

A handful of salts – sea salt or glacier salt

A small handful of jasmine flowers

A few drops of frankincense oil

A few drops of jasmine oil

A few drops of sweet orange oil

A cinnamon stick

What to do:

* Pound the resins to a powder in a mortar and pestle.
* Add these to a bowl along with the rest of the ingredients and stir deosil with the cinnamon stick. Store in an airtight jar. Use three tablespoons in your bath when you need some extra power and shine!

Spell for Success

This is a simple spell but there are powerful, strong and ancient magickal traditions built into it.

YOU'LL NEED:
A gold candle
A key
A cinnamon stick
A golden charm pouch

WHAT TO DO:

❋ On a Sunday, go to your altar and open your circle.

❋ Call in each of the elements.

❋ Using your index finger, cast a circle of light around yourself, tracing it in the air anti-clockwise. See a beautiful circle of white light protecting, balancing and energising you and your magickal space. Say:

I welcome the spirits of the earth, air, fire and water
to this circle. Blessed be!

❋ Take the candle. Carve your name and the word 'successful' into it. Add any details you may wish such as success at school or a new job. You can get as detailed as you want.

❋ Take your candle and hold it up towards the sun. If it is a sunny day you may wish to do this working in a safe space outside to feel the sun's rays on your body and in your magick. If it is not possible for you to be outside, simply see and feel the sun's rays. Say:

> *By Athena, Apollo and Aphrodite*
> *My success now ignited via thee*
> *By all the power of three times three*
> *As I do will, so mote it be.*

❀   Feel the sun's powerful magickal energy pouring into your gold
candle. Place it on the altar and light it, feeling your success come
alive. Take your key and hold it to the sun. Say:

> *By Athena, Apollo and Aphrodite*
> *To my success I now hold the key*
> *By all the power of three times three*
> *As I do will, so mote it be.*

❀   Place your key on your altar with the gold candle. As you do so, feel
the power of your success spell moving out into the world. Take your
cinnamon stick and hold it to the sun. Say:

> *By Athena, Apollo and Aphrodite*
> *Success so sweet now comes to me*
> *By all the powers of three times three*
> *As I do will, so mote it be.*

❀   Place your cinnamon stick on your altar along with your key and candle.
As you do so, understand that whatever comes to you is for the highest
good of all concerned and that this success will serve your happiness.
❀   Stand with your arms outstretched and feel the energy
of the sun pouring into you, lighting up your very cells
and activating all your potential for success.

❋ Say out loud in a strong, clear voice three times:

I am a radiant, successful being.

❋ When your candle has burned down take its wax, your key and cinnamon and place all three together in your gold charm pouch. Tie the cord three times. As you do so say:

Bound around this spell shall be
By all the powers of three times three
True, my success now comes to me
As I do will, so mote it be.

❋ Thank and farewell the elements. Say:

Farewell and thank you, elements of earth, air,
fire, water and spirit.

❋ Close your magick circle by pointing your index finger in the direction you began in and trace your circle clockwise, drawing the beautiful energy of the circle back into you.

❋ Ground yourself by eating something healthy and drink plenty of water.

❋ Carry your charm pouch on you for the rest of Sunday's daylight hours.

❋ On Sunday evening, take your key out of the pouch and wear it around your neck for at least one week. You may wear it longer if you wish, but be sure to wear it until the following Sunday at the same time you put it on to fully activate its magick. If it cannot be worn as a necklace, simply carry the key in your pocket or tuck it into your bra!

Charge Up My Path Spell

YOU'LL NEED:

A candle, undyed

Some scissors or a boline

Your Grimoire and a pen

WHAT TO DO:

* Cast your circle.
* Chant three or nine times the following:

Power, courage, clarity

As I do will, so mote it be

I cast this circle in time and space

The guardians enter now this place

Open circle, hold within

Power swelling into being.

* Sitting in your sacred space, breathe in deeply. Feel the presence of the great void from which the Goddesses can move and join you in your own circle. Say with great sincerity:

Artemis, Hestia, Hecate

From this sacred circle

I call to thee

I ask you all to join me now

I wish to ask you truly, how

My life can be strong, bright and free

Self-determined, made by me
A life that's full of love and health
Courage, peace and well-earned wealth
I await your presence, I call your names
I offer you my Self this day.

❋ Light the candle and gaze into it for three deep breaths, in and out.

❋ Cut a little of your hair and burn it in the candle fire.

This way Goddesses will know you. Say out loud:

Artemis, your arrow it will fly
Straight and true across the sky
Help me aim my own like yours
Across the forest, across the shores
Let my purpose be strong and clean
I seek to know what it is I mean
To know myself in deepest dark
To understand what's in my heart
To care for my Self and know my needs
To feel no guilt when these I seek
I ask for hounds to protect me now
For stag to come, to show me how
I create all that I am
From this place such freedom sprang
That I will go forth and make my life
What it will be, in darkness and light
I will hunt for what I must
I will satisfy my lust
For a life that's free and wild and strong
Artemis, know that I belong
To forest deep and clean bright sight
I begin this work with you tonight.

❖ Write down a promise to your own self. Imagine for a moment your young self coming to you – as Artemis, bright, maiden, free, wild. What advice would she give you? What advice can she share? Say out loud:

Hestia for my home and hearth
From sacred meals and purifying bath
Instil in me the urge to make
A home that nurtures, so I create
All that I need and wish to be
A bed where sleep will come to me
A place where tree and faery roam
A place that is my own soul home
Food that's fresh of fruit and vine
A little bread, salt and wine
Enough for me to go within
And restore each day anew begin.

❖ See Hestia coming to you as Mother. She is nurturing, kind and wishes to support you. What advice does she give you? What insights can she offer? Write these down. Say out loud:

Hestia, I ask you light my way
The crossroads that I face each day
Help me step onto my true path
Help me learn to choose between
The things that seem but are not good for me
Wisdom of your torch please shine
Into the dark spaces, where I'll divine
With your help what is best for me
And even in darkness I will see
Clear my way! Break new ground!
Strength, independence, I have found!

Let the fires purify
Anything that I desire
Which may not be truly good for me
As I do will, so mote it be!

❋ See Hecate come to you: crone, older, wiser self who has
seen all the choices before you. What has she to say to you?
What insights can she offer you? Write these down.

❋ When you have done this, sincerely thank all of the Goddesses. Offer each
one of them something from yourself. It can be some fruit, a little cake,
something delicious. Offer to clear an area from litter for Artemis, for
Hestia it may be to nurture your own self more, to Hecate to ask her to
shine the light and respect her assistance and to light a candle to her for a
time, and for those candles to be ones that are clear and non-toxic. Say:

The power of this spell within me
As I do will, so mote it be
As I do will, so mote it be
As I do will, so mote it be.

❋ It is time to thank and farewell this circle for now. Snuff the candle. Trace
the circle round in the opposite direction to that which you cast it in (so,
clockwise) saying:

My circle is open, but never is it broken. My circle is open,
but never is it broken.

❋ Take a moment to breathe and feel the energy shifting.

A Glossary of Magickal Terms and Tools

Asatru Traditional Nordic system of magick with cultural and philosophical influence and impact. Includes the use of runes and stav, an ancient Northern European form of self-defence.

Athame A double-bladed Witch's knife with a black handle. Used to work with energy, cut through cords, sever energetic connections and create doorways into dimensions or other planes and realms. It never cuts anything on the material plane.

Bane Poison, toxin; a woeful, unwanted energy that turns all to loss and ruin.

Bell A bell is used to clear space or to call on certain elementals. Faeries are particularly drawn to bells.

Bend To shape material reality in accord with natural laws so they merge with the will.

Besom A Witch's broom that is used to clear and uplift energy, made and shaped magickally.

Bind To magickally restrict the potential or urge to harm or hurt.

Black magick Whether magick is evil or malicious or kind or healthy is really about the purpose of the spell and the intention of the caster. There is no black or white – it is all about the focus and energy of the intention and action.

Boline A white-handled Witch's knife with a crescent blade that is used to cut herbs and plants.

Book of Shadows, Book of Shadows and Light When wicca was revived in the 20th century, Gerald Gardner created the term 'Book of Shadows' to refer to a Witch's book of magickal notes, castings, symbols and formulas. A 'Book of Shadows and Light' is the term I created to refer to a book that is the same but is not always secret or shadowy, so it is both dark and light.

Candle magick A form of magick that works with flame and light. Candles are dedicated to a particular purpose, and the burning of them activates the spell.

Cast The action of sending out magick.

Cast a circle To create a circular space of protection or healing. A world between the worlds in which magick can safely be practised, a threshold that contains magick in a safe space, a threshold across which negativity cannot pass.

Cauldron A cast-iron, three-legged Witch's cauldron can be used to cook, brew potions or hold fire for a ritual.

Charmstone A stone or crystal that has been blessed and charged with energy for a magickal purpose. It can then be held, dipped in water or touched to pass the blessing or the magick along. It is a traditional practice in Scotland, Ireland, Northern England and Iceland and amid the indigenous tribal peoples of the Americas.

Circle A gathering of Witches or spiritually inclined people. The circle is formed in order to avoid hierarchy. Circles are without beginning and end, top or bottom.

Cloutie This is the old word for ribbons or sometimes strips of fabric that are tied to trees connected to powerful healing energies, the Gods and Goddesses of the land and the sacred wells. Many cloutie trees are found near holy wells, like those of Madron Well in Cornwall.

Colour magick Hues hold vibration and have an energetic, psychological and physiological impact on us. Colours can add magick to all our spells and help hold the magick in place.

BLACK: for banishing – tie your ribbon during the waning moon or when the weather turns colder and winter begins to make her chilly presence felt.

WHITE: for spiritual assistance – increasing intuition, for example.

RED: for passion and love.

BLUE: for harmonious communication and friendship.

GREEN: for growth and connection to nature, healthy bodies and minds.

PURPLE: for royalty, higher states, connection to all.

Coven A group of Witches who are committed to raising energy, working magick and developing their powers together through regular collective work, ceremony and spellcasting. Structure, hierarchy and frequency of gatherings varies from coven to coven.

Curse Ill-wishing, purposely desiring harm to another and taking steps to achieve this.

Deosil Sun-wise. In the northern hemisphere this is clockwise, as the sun rises in the east and moves to the south. Sun-wise in the southern hemisphere is anti-clockwise as the sun rises in the east and moves to the north. This direction is expansive, opening and a calling in.

Dowsing The practice of dowsing using a dowsing rod. A dowsing rod is Y-shaped, made of wood or iron (willow, copper or bronze being common) to trace the energy lines running beneath the earth, often known as ley lines. Dowsing can also be used to trace and locate elements such as water or items that are lost.

Drawing down the moon A powerful wiccan ritual in which a woman is inhabited by the spirit of the Goddess for a portion of the rite in order for others to have direct communication with the feminine Divine. The magickal words used by the priest and priestess to draw down the moon (bring the Goddess into the body of the Witch) are often the Charge of the Goddess, a modern invocation.

Druid An ancient British spiritual order or practitioner. Druids were the storytellers, poets, musicians, lawkeepers, teachers and advisers of pre-Roman Britain, Ireland and many parts of Western Europe, including northern Spain and western France.

Egregore An energy intentionally or unintentionally formed by a gathering of people that can take on its own independent life. The egregore can be given a magickal mission. Some last for only a short time, others endure for aeons.

Esbat A Witches' gathering held outside the eight festivals of the Wheel of the Year.

Familiar A gifted animal companion that works with a spellcaster to enhance their magick. They are part of the spellcaster's family and are respected, consulted and connected with.

Fith fath An energetic form created to dispatch your magickal work to another location or at another time; for example, when you are sleeping or otherwise occupied the fith fath can do the magickal work.

Glamour The art of changing appearance at will, or changing another's perception of you at will.

Grimoire An instruction book of magick and spellcraft that contains the personal notes and rites of magicians, Witches or magickal practitioners.

Hail A term of greeting, as in 'Hail and welcome!' Directions, elements, Goddesses and Gods are often greeted this way when circle is cast.

Handfasting A traditional pagan commitment ceremony to bind two people in a formal relationship that would last for a year and one day. It is called handfasting for the fabrics or ribbons that would gently bind the hands of both partners.

Hex A spell or rite that is worked with malintent.

Incantation A series of words chanted over and over to raise power and direct magickal energy.

Initiate An initiate is a person who is undergoing magickal training, after which they will be tested through ceremony, quest or ritual. If their training manifests during the test they are then welcomed into the organisation, coven or establishment.

Invoke To ask for the God or Goddess or a particular being or energy to manifest during a spell or ceremony. Often used interchangeably with evoke, although to evoke is a more subtle, less intense and direct experience.

Juju A magick of the traditions of West Africa.

Kumina Ecstatic dancing and drumming rites indigenous to Jamaica.

Madron Mother, a female leader of wisdom and many years, or Great Mother Goddess. A madron is also a female leader in Druid orders.

Megalith Massive neolithic stone temples and monuments such as Stonehenge and Avebury.

Menhir Breton word for standing stone.

Mesmer The art of hypnotising, capturing the power of another person's will.

Mojo Sex magick, the art of working with sex appeal. A magickal charm or conjure that supports sex appeal.

Necromancy The art of divining by communing with the dead. Its modern-day variation is mediumship.

Neopagan The modern practice of paganism.

Ogham An Irish alphabet based on sacred trees; a system of divination.

Oracle An intermediary between the Divine and the human worlds. Modern oracles include card readers or psychics. Oracles in the past include the priestesses of Apollo at Delphi in Greece.

Ovate A seer, prophet, able to foresee the future and read the signs of nature. Druidic in origin.

Pagan From the word *paganus*, meaning 'country dweller', this word is used to describe those who follow an earth-based spiritual path that stands outside organised religion and its doctrines.

Pantheon A high-ranking collective of deities; for example, the Greek pantheon of twelve primary Gods and Goddesses.

Pendulum The use of a crystal or weight attached to a chain or thread that is asked to provide 'Yes' or 'No' answers. The pendulum swings in the direction of the answer.

Pentacle The pentacle is a Pythagorean form, a five-pointed star enclosed within a circle. It represents earth, air, fire, water and spirit in balance.

Poppet A doll representing a person or persons upon whom magick is to be worked. Often used in binding spells or to enhance magick. There is a long history of sacred dolls that hold magick and possess powers.

Potion A potion is a kind of drink that is made with magickal intentions and magickal ingredients for a specific purpose. They can also work on a vibrational level and include sacred or blessed waters.

Querent A person who has a question requiring a magickal or spiritual response. A seeker who wishes to find answers and who may seek help from a divination session.

Quimbanda The indigenous magick of Brazil.

Rede A code, a declaration, as in the Wiccan Rede.

Ritual A ceremony with a particular order and set structure, often with several participants. Magickal rituals are often held to celebrate the Wheel of the Year and its festivals to raise energy for healing or to create, experience and activate the sacred.

Runes An ancient Nordic system of stark, linear symbols that have mundane, philosophical and oracular meanings and significance. Runes can be worked with to enhance spellwork, attract energy and protect the user from harm. They form a true body of magickal work.

Sabbat A Witches' gathering to celebrate the rites of one of the eight festivals of the Wheel of the Year.

Scry The art of divination through gazing, such as when a gypsy stares into a crystal ball. Scrying can also be performed by entering a light trance and staring into fire, a still body of water, clouds or a dark piece of glass. It is an ancient art that shifts perception in order to receive messages from beyond the human realm.

Shaman A Siberian word that has been used widely to describe wise men and women who are the keepers of indigenous practices of magick and ritual.

Sigil Creating a sigil is a form of magick, where a symbol is created by the spellcaster to hold the energy of the desired outcome.

Skyclad Nudity in spellcraft, rituals or magick. Not sexual, but a way of deeply entering into nature and being utterly revealed, vulnerable, transparent – and free.

Strega The Italian word for 'witch'. Stregheria is the Italian traditional practice of the craft.

Tarot A divination system using cartomancy featuring 78 cards divided into three sections: the major and minor arcanas and the court cards. There are four suits with prescribed meanings. With its mysterious origins the tarot is a gateway into archetypes, a complete system of magick and an effective way of predicting events and outcomes.

Undine A magickal being who belongs to the element of water.

Vesica piscis A sacred symbol consisting of two circles that intersect equally.

Vodou The religious practice and tradition that merges folk magick, witchcraft and the Catholicism of Haiti. It has variations around the world and originated in East Africa. Variations include Louisiana voodoo, Santeria and Candomblé.

Wand A wand directs energy and can be made of wood, bone, stone, iron or crystal. They have their own energy and are often used to cast circles to heal or to pour energy into an object or person.

White Witch There is no real white or black magick. It's a question of the character of the person doing the casting and their motivation, intent and the actions they choose to take.

Wicca The modern reconstruction of ancient witchcraft.

Wicce Anglo Saxon word meaning 'to bend' and 'to shape', and 'wisdom'.

Widdershins To direct against the sun – the opposite direction to deosil. In the northern hemisphere this is anti-clockwise – from east to north to west. In the southern hemisphere it is from the east, to the south, to the west then to the north again. We cast circle or work or stir in this direction to clear, banish and separate, or to close or unwind a circle that has been cast for group or solo spellwork.

Magickal Ingredients

Let's see what you'll need to stock up on to begin your crafting and casting. Some of your magickal supplies can come from the supermarket, others can come from magickal websites and you may wish to purchase some from a New Age or occult store. These can be wonderful soulful stores where you can meet some friendly and helpful like-minded people – like nearly everything, it's about whether the place feels right to you. The kinds of places that resonate with me tend to be big on books, old magickal paraphernalia and free will and a little light on tie-dye and rainbows and unsolicited advice – not that there is anything at all wrong with tie-dye and rainbows. It's just not my thing as much as wood and wands and herbs that are handpicked and dried. The personal touch really matters in spellcrafting and casting as you're going to be working with energy, and the energy with which something is made . . . well, I feel it counts because I've seen the influence and impact the origins can have. Having said that, you can always attune anything you buy to your own energy by giving it a cleanse and a clear, then charging it with your intention and energy. Anyway: to the list! It's fun going shopping for magickal goods and I hope you find some wonderful quirky objects and pieces that really support your magick.

Essential oils

Essential oils are nothing short of amazing as they are pure plant magick. A little further along the track you might want to explore flower essences, but for me the incredible power of oils is just so effective and the results are so immediate. Pure essential oils derived from plants are not perfume, so be careful when you buy your oils that you're buying oil and not cheap imitations or essences that have been diluted with water or other base oils. Always check the labels and go for the 100 per cent pure essential oils. You don't need to purchase oil blends because you can make your own blends at a fraction of the cost, and you can make it really personal by mixing in some of your own energy.

To choose oils, test some and see what you really love. You might want to invest in a good range of oils. For starters, here are some essential oils that are a good base for blends and for using in spellcasting. You will probably end up working with them most days: *lavender, sweet orange, bergamot, rose geranium, rosewood*.

And if you have the money, you might want to invest – and it is an investment – in *frankincense and sandalwood*.

Each oil will have its own special characteristics that come to you directly from the healing and medical energies and properties of the plant. What I truly love about essential oils is how sensual it feels working with them. As soon as you open that bottle, the beautiful aroma will enter your bloodstream via your nose. Place them on your skin (in blends) and they enter your bloodstream. And I love flower essences, too, the energy and the way they work (real gentle and subtle, but very strong) but my dilemma with many of them is that they have alcohol in them as a preservative. I don't drink and I find the taste and smell of alcohol repulsive, so essences are a bit tricky for me. Essential oils are where it's at for magickal work, I feel.

Consecrated water

Well, that's easy, right? Straight out of the tap? Can we just stop and think about this for a second. I'd like you to collect and store a few different types of water. Water is a beautiful element — it holds a lot of energy, a lot of memory, of individuals and of groups, and water is really powerful for this reason. It also can have a bit of a downside in that it can as effectively store and hold energy that isn't healthy just as much as it can hold and store really beautiful, flowing, positive energy.

What you'll need to do is find a healthy, positive body of water near you. Now, this could be a river or a lake or the ocean. It could be a pond or creek, but it is not going to be a swimming pool or a communal spa! It could be that you don't have natural flowing bodies of water like rivers and oceans or lakes near you or you just don't have any way of getting out to them. In that case, rainwater is fantastic, especially if collected under moonlight — the phase of the moon will have a direct influence on the energy you're holding in the water.

Once you've collected your water I'd like you to charge it. Charging is the act of empowering it, programming it with a particular kind of energy. Here's how to charge this water. Get into a good emotional space — feel great, feel powerful, feel strong and amazing. Pick up your bottle of water and let the energy flow from you into the water. Whatever it is that you most desire in your life, really feel it in the present moment. No negative thoughts, no 'This is wishful thinking.' For the highest good of all concerned, just ponder those things as if they are already yours. The more you believe this the better your results will be.

Label your water — mine (I have about 10 jars of water going) are labelled hilariously 'eclipse 2012', 'new moon, new year 2013', 'Beltane morning dew', 'rainwater under dark moon' with the date and so on. Over time you'll have an awesome collection of energy stored via your blessed waters and you'll be able to use it. Think of this as a collection of fluid batteries, charged and ready to go to work to enhance the energy of your castings!

Candles

You are going to need candles! Tea lights are sort of okay, but my preference is for beeswax or for soy as their energy is beautiful, earth-loving and burning them ionises your atmosphere, making it feel uplifting, plus they also improve the quality of the air. Paraffin wax candles don't do that. If tea lights from the supermarket are all you can get, that is fine for the moment. In time, however, I would recommend finding a beekeeper or someone who makes their own candles – there are plenty of these folk around and it's a great thing to support such skilled, energetic artisans. Sometimes I recommend a coloured candle, but most times I will not. You can buy ethically made coloured candles, too, so shop around. The better the energy, the better your casting.

An oil burner
Buy a good-quality oil burner that will safely hold water and your oils.

Flameproof container
This could be a cauldron, mini-cauldron, terracotta tile, incense burner . . . your choice! Remember op shops and Etsy, the handmade online marketplace, are excellent places to get your supplies from, as well as the local occult or magickal store.

Matches
Far better than a gas lighter, energetically speaking, and kinder to the environment.

Charcoal discs
You can make your own charcoal. Not many folks do as it is too time-consuming. However, there are brands of charcoal that are environmentally friendly. Shop around.

Tweezers
Unless your fingertips are insensitive, you will need these to hold your charcoal while you light it. It will help you avoid that dropping-the-charcoal moment during your spellcasting that interrupts you, throws you off track and singes your fingers.

Sea salt, lake salt or glacier salt
Your call, but buy a good, strong, really close to the source salt – not one of those finely ground supermarket kinds. The more natural it is the more it will work an absolute treat in your spellcasting and purification rituals. If you go to a good wholefoods store you can often buy salt a lot cheaper than you can in the supermarket.

Crystals
This can get expensive if you are going to New Age stores to buy your crystals. There are some really wonderful wholesalers around and if you look on Facebook or even on ebay there are people re-selling crystals. Be aware that most crystals have been mined, which

means they tend to have been dynamited or exploded out of the ground. This is a high-impact industry that creates traumatised stones (yes, they are). So I would choose my crystals well, and use them powerfully, and mindfully. And I would also thank the earth for offering you this incredible energy amplifier. And keep an eye out – I gather my own stones in modest amounts – and I thank the earth for them and treat them very well. Some of my most powerful stone pieces are from places where the earth holds a great deal of energy such as my stones from Merlin's cave in Cornwall. They are strong – just like their wizard namesake.

Herbs

Grow your own, or if you have a good local farmer's market you'll be amazed at what magickal herbs are available. I love to have bay leaf, juniper berries and black pepper on hand, and cinnamon sticks and powder are always readily available from supermarkets and spice shops. Explore the spice aisle and see what calls to you.

Your own Grimoire and a pen you love using

This is your magickal journal in which you can write your private thoughts about magick, rituals, the moon, your spells and your every thought about the enchanted life you're creating. Customise it and make it a perfect reflection of who you are at this time.